Velvet Paws & Whiskers

Velvet Paws & Whiskers

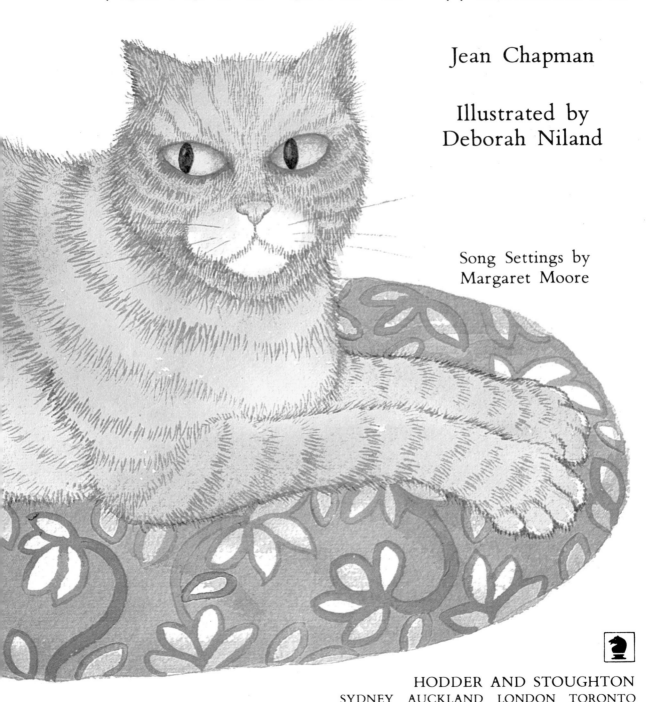

Jean Chapman

Illustrated by
Deborah Niland

Song Settings by
Margaret Moore

HODDER AND STOUGHTON
SYDNEY AUCKLAND LONDON TORONTO

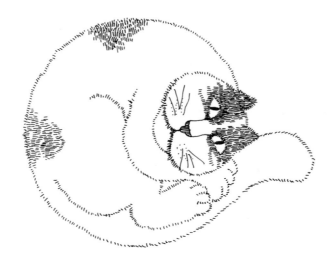

First published in 1979
by Hodder and Stoughton (Australia) Pty Limited,
2 Apollo Place, Lane Cove, NSW 2066
In association with
Hodder and Stoughton Children's Books,
Mill Road, Dunton Green, Sevenoaks, Kent.

National Library of Australia Cataloguing-in-Publication entry
Velvet paws and whiskers
  Index.
  For Children.
  ISBN 0 340 24605 7
  I. Chapman, Jean, comp. II. Niland, Deborah, illus
  III. Moore, Margaret

Typeset by G.T. Setters Pty Ltd, Lane Cove
Printed in Hong Kong

INTRODUCTION

Many centuries ago; it is not known exactly when, *Felis domestica* took up his place in the human household. It was probably a cave at the time, as prehistoric cave paintings depicting cats, in what are thought to be domestic situations, have been found. So cats have been part of human family life for almost all of man's history and, to families which include a cat, it is impossible to imagine it otherwise.

Very few cats have worked for their living as many other animals that live with man are required to do. More often they have moved into a household of their choosing and trained the humans. Generally, they have spent quiet, pampered lives, perhaps catching the odd mouse or rat — a favourite pastime, rather than a chore.

Although cats and man have lived together for so long, cats have managed to retain an air of dignity and aloofness which renders them slightly mysterious to mere humans. In fact, throughout history cats have been accredited with many special powers. The Ancient Egyptians worshipped the cat Goddess Bast, and treated their household cats with great esteem.

It was not until the Dark ages that humans developed a superstitious fear of cats and believed they possessed evil and sinister powers. Cats were associated with witches and their secret rituals, sometimes even being burned at the stake with their mistresses! It was probably from these beliefs that many of the superstitous sayings we know today originated.

So it is not surprising that a whole body of literature about cats has developed over the centuries — grown out of all the legends — featuring cats in all their moods, using all their legendary powers. Children's literature also abounds in cat characters. Cats are the most cunning, imaginative, intelligent, independent and steadfast of all creatures. Who could imagine a more cunning animal than a cat in PUSS IN BOOTS? or a more loyal servant for DICK WHITTINGTON? or a more graceful and adoring bride in THE OWL AND THE PUSSYCAT?

One may wonder when it will all end — whether there is room for yet another book about cats. It is obvious that this book was compiled by cat lovers. It cannot fail to take its place in many cat libraries and so become a worthy addition to the literature of cats.

Margaret Hamilton

Dedication

For
The Altschwagers, the Hamiltons, the Steers
other families owned by sleek cats
and for you too

and also for
Mango and William

CONTENTS

Key to Symbols for contents
◔ = story   ◔ = verse
⊛ = activity   ♫ = song

◔ Spring Is Coming		11
◔ A Wondrous Thing		12
⊛ Cats' Cradle		15
◔ Most Beautiful And Most Precious		16
♫ Little Bird		19
◔ Cat		20
⊛ Cat Toys		20
⊛ Tabby Teasers		22
♫ Kitty Alone	*Traditional song, England*	24
◔ Tillica		25
◔ Wash First, Then Eat	*Traditional tale from Arabia*	26
⊛ Cat Bath		29
◔ Mother Shuttle		30
♫ At-Choom!		31
◔ A Place By The Fire	*Traditional tale from India*	32
⊛ Pussy Wants A Corner		35
⊛ Cat Comfort		36
◔ Cat Naps		37
⊛ Cat's Pyjamas		38
◔ Conversation In The Middle Of The Night		40
◔ Pillowcase Cat	*Aesop*	41
◔ Belling The Cat	*Aesop*	42
♫ The Old Grey Cat		43

◌ ROOSTER KING *Traditional African tale*		44
♫ BARNYARD SONG *Traditional American song*		48
✿ CLUCKY HEN		50
◌ NINE LIVES		50
✿ THE CAT'S DINNER		51
◌ ANYTHING FOR FISH		52
✿ HERE IS THE SEA		55
◌ FAT CAT		56
♫ I KNOW AN OLD LADY *Traditional American song*		62
◌ DEVIL-MOUSE *Traditional Latvian tale*		64
✿ NOAH'S ARK		67
◌ WHERE'S YOUR TAIL, PUSSY?		68
◌ TAILS		74
◌ NANCY'S CAT		75
✿ KNITTING NANCY		79
✿ CLICKITY-CLICK!		80
◌ SWISH GOES THE BROOMSTICK!		83
◌ VELVET PAWS		84
✿ A SPELL FOR GOOD LUCK		88
✿ WITCH'S BREW		89
✿ PUPPET WITCH		90
✿ PEANUT PUPPETS		90
✿ SOCK PUPPET		91
◌ KILKENNY CATS *Traditional nursery rhyme*		91
◌ TWO RED, ROUND CAKES *Traditional tale from Japan*		92
♫ JUBA		94
◌ CATS' EYES		95
◌ THE BOY WHO DREW CATS		97
✿ DRAW OR PAINT		101

🐱 CLEVER TOM   *Traditional from Indonesia*   102

🐾 MONKEY BUSINESS   104

🎵 LONG TIME AGO   *Traditional English song*   105

🐱 KING SOLOMON'S RING   106

🐱 THE ROSE IS RED   109

🐱 THE OWL AND THE PUSSY-CAT   110

🐾 BEANS IN A BAG   112

🎵 THE CAT CAME BACK   113

🐱 THE MAGIC RING   115

🐾 CAT AND DOG GAME   119

🐱 THERE WAS A CROOKED MAN   120

🐾 FUN-MOUSE   121

🐱 TAILOR MOUSE   123

🐱 SIX LITTLE MICE   126

🐱 MOUSE-HOUND   127

🎵 OLD MOTHER MITCHELL   *Traditional French song*   132

🐱 DICK WHITTINGTON   133

🐾 RING-A-LING!   140

🐱 DING-DONG!   142

🐱 THE BELLS OF LONDON   143

🐱 KURREMURRE   *Traditional Danish tale*   144

🐱 PUSSICAT, WUSSICAT   149

🐾 ROLL-ABOUT TROLLS   149

🎵 LOVE SOMEBODY   150

🐾 GIVE A HEART   151

🐱 LORD OF THE GOLDEN UMBRELLAS   *Traditional Siamese tale*   152

🐾 CATTY SAYINGS   156

🐱 PUSS IN BOOTS   *Traditional French tale*   158

🐾 CAT IN A BOOT   166

   INDEX   168

SPRING IS COMING

Spring is coming,
Spring is coming!
How do I know?
Found some pussy willows;
I know it must be so.

A WONDROUS THING

Long, long ago, no one knows where and no one knows when, a grey farm cat had a litter of kittens. She hid them in a corner of a dark shed. These were not the first, not the last kittens to be hidden so. That has always been the way of cats.

The kittens were very like any breed of new kitten that you may have been lucky enough to see. Tiny, frail, sprawling, grey mewlings with tightly closed eyes. They were feeble and they were helpless, and the farmer, not wanting more cats about, hunted until he found them. Four tiny cats! He scooped them up into his hat then strode out of the shed to the river. The Mother Cat followed anxiously, mewing her concern to him.

The farmer ignored her cries. He threw the kittens into the river as if they were stones, then he went back to his house.

Their mother was frantic. She ran crying along the bank. Scratching! Clawing! Desperately she tried to find a way down the banks which were as steep as walls. She couldn't reach the water and her mews were pitious. Her voice grew high and thin with grief. The birds stopped singing. Bees stopped buzzing. Grasshoppers stopped clicking wings. In their silence, it was as if all creatures were listening to the cat's wails for her kittens.

Now, on the far bank of the river grew a row of trees with slim branches which trailed leaves towards the water. And, as if the trees had seen the kittens' plight, their branches drooped lower and lower into the river. Long slender stems and narrow leaves ribboned outwards towards the kittens, to dip and twist under the small struggling bodies, to overlap and weave a floating cradle of leaves.

Kittens' paws grasped at twigs and stems. Kittens' paws clung tightly to the leaf-cradle. It floated them down the stream.

Eagerly the Mother Cat scrambled along the bank, keeping pace with the rescued kittens. She mewed soft, encouraging little sounds until the kittens reached the shallows, below the clump of river trees. Here the cliff-bank fell away to a crossing.

A sure-footed leap and the Cat crossed to her kittens, then one by one, by the scruff of its neck, she carried each one ashore.

She made a nest for her kittens in the roots of the trees. And it was a well-hidden, low-down, hide-away, secret nest which no one ever found.

The kittens grew into cats and as summer passed into winter, the leaves of the river-bank trees turned from green to gold. Then autumn winds stripped the branches bare for winter's cold.

When spring came the glossy buds swelling on the branches did not burst to unfold new leaves as had happened in other years. Instead, each branch was shyly decked with grey blossoms, blossoms as sleek as kitten's fur. Never before had the trees flowered.

Each year since the same flowers have appeared.

No one knows where and no one knows when the trees were first called Pussy Willows but they still grow well in watery places. Should you have the chance, feel the little catkin bud. And that will be a wondrous thing for you.

CATS' CRADLE

Eskimos may have invented the game of Cats' Cradle and shared it with children everywhere, because it is played about the world. Its name may have come from an old word, *cratch* which was a name for a manger, a feeding box for farm animals. Who knows? Play Cats' Cradle alone or with others and you are sure to learn other patterns to make with your length of string, wool or yarn.

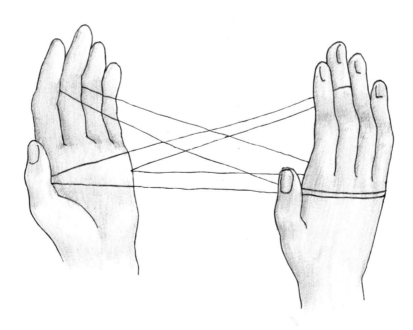

MOST BEAUTIFUL AND MOST PRECIOUS

Once, when the world was young, a black cat caught a
fledgling, a little goldfinch. He was about to gobble up the
baby bird when its mother fluttered from a branch to circle
about the cat's head, crying and crying, "Oh, Gracious Cat!
Most Splendid Puss! Let my child live! He is the most
beautiful and the most precious of birds!"

"Spppt!" hissed Black Cat through his mouthful of
feathers. "Precious! Beautiful! All birds taste the same and
I'm going to chew this one up."

"Don't! Please, *please!* I'll bring you another bird in his
place."

"You will?" smirked Black Cat and he thought, "I'll
have *two* birds for dinner then." And he was smart enough
to keep that thought to himself. "You will?" he mumbled.

"I will. I *will!*" she promised.

"Flap off then," snarled Black Cat. "I'm hungry, hungry,
hungry. Hungry enough to eat you, too!"

The goldfinch flew away. She flew and flew until she

16

met Sparrow. "Sparrow, good Sparrow! Your children are plain and grey like fire ash," she said. "Give me one so that Black Cat may eat it."

Sparrow shrieked. She fluffed her feathers. She flapped her wings. She pecked at Goldfinch. "My children are a hundred times more beautiful and more precious than yours," she screamed. "Fly off, you-good-for-nothing-feather-duster! Go before I peck your eyes!"

Goldfinch flew away. She flew and flew until she met Raven. "Raven, noble Raven! Your children are plain and black like dull night," she said. "Give me one so that Black Cat may eat it."

Raven croaked, too shocked to speak, then she cawed, "Are you mad? My children are a thousand times more beautiful and more precious than yours. Be off, or I'll snap your legs with my beak."

Goldfinch flew away. She flew and flew until she met Owl. "Owl, wise Owl! Your children are plain and strangely shaped. Give me one so that Black Cat may eat it."

Owl hooted. *She hooted!* She hooted, "My children are a million times more beautiful and more precious than yours!" Then Owl could hoot no more. She was near choking with anger. She gathered herself up to look twice her size, then lunged off her branch in a swooping attack at Goldfinch.

Again, Goldfinch flew away. She flew slowly now. So slowly! She could think of no way to save her child. No way!

Then, strange as it may be, Goldfinch began to fly faster. She came diving in, over Black Cat to hover with whirring wings above his head. "Eat *me! Eat me!*" she sang. "Let my child live. *Eat me!*"

"I'll eat you *both*," he smirked up at her and sprang into the air with clutching paws, forgetting to hold the baby goldfinch.

Swoooooosh! The little bird fluttered upwards, up and up to join his mother circling above Black Cat's head. Then higher and higher flew the two birds, away from the prancing cat. Goodness only knows what he ate for dinner that day. It was *not* goldfinch. *It was not!*

LITTLE BIRD

Lit - tle bird, fly a - way! Old cat's hunt - ing birds to - day.

Lit - tle bird, fly a - way, Fly, fly, fly, fly, fly a - way.

19

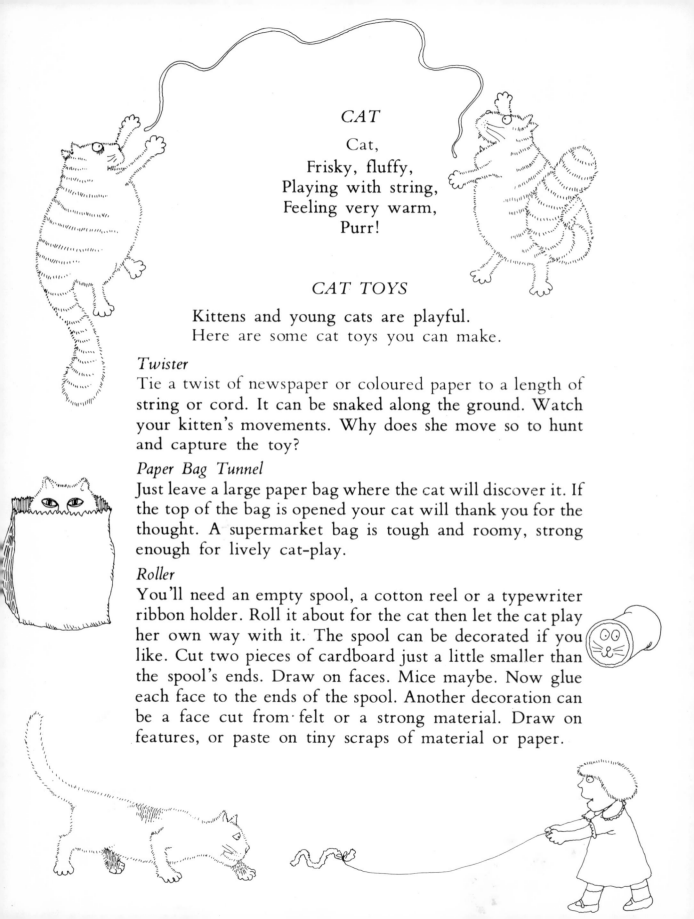

CAT

Cat,
Frisky, fluffy,
Playing with string,
Feeling very warm,
Purr!

CAT TOYS

Kittens and young cats are playful.
Here are some cat toys you can make.

Twister

Tie a twist of newspaper or coloured paper to a length of string or cord. It can be snaked along the ground. Watch your kitten's movements. Why does she move so to hunt and capture the toy?

Paper Bag Tunnel

Just leave a large paper bag where the cat will discover it. If the top of the bag is opened your cat will thank you for the thought. A supermarket bag is tough and roomy, strong enough for lively cat-play.

Roller

You'll need an empty spool, a cotton reel or a typewriter ribbon holder. Roll it about for the cat then let the cat play her own way with it. The spool can be decorated if you like. Cut two pieces of cardboard just a little smaller than the spool's ends. Draw on faces. Mice maybe. Now glue each face to the ends of the spool. Another decoration can be a face cut from felt or a strong material. Draw on features, or paste on tiny scraps of material or paper.

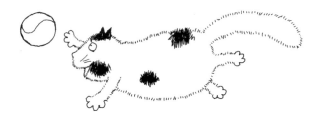

Cat Ball

A crumpled ball of rustling paper is all you need. Or give your cat an old tennis ball, or a ping-pong ball. The ping-pong ball won't last very long.

Moonface

Moonface is made from two small circles of brightly coloured felt or vinyl. Cut them to about the size of a large coin. Stitch them firmly together and trim the edges with pinking-shears if you like. Draw on a moon face with a felt pen. Sew a tiny joy bell to one edge and a short length of hat elastic opposite the bell. The toy can be hung from a chair leg or a door handle by the elastic but if a magnet is tied on the end it can dangle from a refrigerator door or some other metal surface.

Other simple shapes such as a fish, a bird, a mouse or a square cushion of cloth also make cat toys. These can be filled with a little dried catnip, a little grey garden plant with a pungent scent which cats like.

Scratching Post

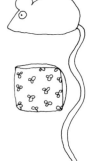

Kittens and cats *must* scratch to wear off the edges of their growing claws just as we trim our finger nails, so that new claws may grow. To avoid scratches on furniture and carpets, an adult will help you to make a scratching post. Find a small log and nail a piece of old carpet to it.

A very posh scratching post can be made by erecting a strong post. Nail carpet to it. Fix a shelf on the top so the cat will have a look-out spot. And if you feel like it, dangle some cat toys from the edge of the shelf. Your cat may need to be shown how to use the scratching post.

TABBY TEASERS

Some grown-ups like to tell Teasers to unsuspecting children. You could trick an adult with one of these. Try it!

First, you find your adult and ask, "Would you like me to tell you a story?" That person is sure to say, "Yes!" And you begin....

This is the story of a Kitten that flicked its tail over its nose, and the Kitten said to a man who passed by, "Would you like me to tell you the story of a Kitten that flicked its tail over its nose", and the Kitten said to a man who passed by, "Would you like me to tell you the story of the kitten that flicked its tail over its nose", and the Kitten said to a man who passed by ...

Keep on repeating these run-around words until the adult realizes your trick, then you'll have to run and escape. Otherwise, you may be grabbed and tickled. Perhaps you'll just enjoy the joke together. And here are some more to remember.

Can a kitten jump as high as a house?

Of course it can! A house can't jump.

What is the use of a cat's skin?

It keeps Pussy's insides together.

What do the children
   In China call
Little yellow cats
   When they are small?

Kittens

As I was going to St Ives,
I met a man with seven wives,
Each wife had seven sacks,
Each sack had seven cats,
Each cat had seven kits,
Kits, cats, sacks and wives,
How many were going to St Ives?

Just the man

Twenty-two tabby kittens sheltered
under Granny Jones' red umbrella.
How many got wet?

None! It wasn't raining!

KITTY ALONE

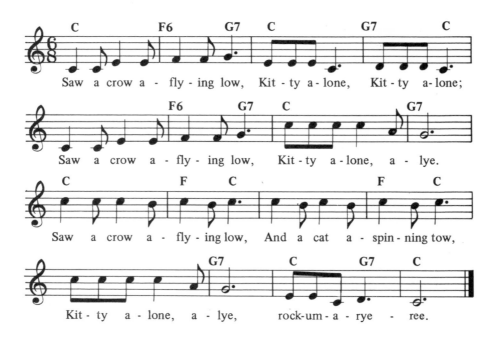

Saw a crow a-fly-ing low, Kit-ty a-lone, Kit-ty a-lone;

Saw a crow a-fly-ing low, Kit-ty a-lone, a-lye.

Saw a crow a-fly-ing low, And a cat a-spin-ning tow,

Kit-ty a-lone, a-lye, rock-um-a-rye-ree.

In came a little cat, kitty alone, kitty alone;
In came a little cat, kitty alone, a-lye.
In came a little cat,
With a piece of mutton fat,
Kitty alone, a-lye, rock-um-a-rye-ree.

Next came in was honeybee, kitty alone, kitty alone;
Next came in was honeybee, kitty alone, a-lye;
Next came in was honeybee,
With a fiddle across his knee,
Kitty alone, a-lye, rock-um-a-rye-ree.

Next came in was little Pete, kitty alone, kitty alone,
Next came in was little Pete, kitty alone, a-lye.
Next came in was little Pete
Thinking about going to sleep,
Kitty alone, a-lye, rock-um-a-rye-ree.

Bee-o, bye-o, baby-o, kitty alone, kitty alone,
Bee-o, bye-o, baby-o, kitty alone, a-lye;
Bee-o, bye-o, baby-o, bye-o, bee-o, baby-o,
Kitty alone, a-lye, rock-um-a-rye-ree.

Almost four hundred years ago Kitty's lullaby was sung in
England. Then it went travelling to the southern states of
America. Now it's yours to sing and to add more verses
about little creatures and people.

TILLICA

Tillica was my kitten
Now she is my cat.
I never did imagine
She'd grow as fast as that!

WASH FIRST, THEN EAT

Siri was prowling about looking for something to eat. Nothing special, mind you, just something tasty for a special cat with long hair and eyes as yellow as a topaz! She looked and looked about the house but saw no mice tracks anywhere. She listened and listened in the garden and heard no bird calls. She sniffed and sniffed about the kitchen and smelt no cream, not even a stinking fish-head. So she went to the garden again. This time she saw a bird pecking up grass-seeds. "Aaaaah!" purred Siri, "a tasty morsel!"

She crouched in the grass, crawled silently through weeds and had that bird between her paws before it had time to flick its tail feathers. *Eeeeeeek!* The bird screeched. It stiffened with shock, unable to move and hardly able to breath.

Worse was to come. Siri twitched her whiskers then pushed and batted at the feathery bird-ball she held. She tormented and teased, sometimes almost letting the bird escape before snatching it back. "I'm going to eat you, feathers and all," Siri mewed.

By then the bird had recovered enough to chirp indignantly, "Surely you will wash first?"

"What? Wash before eating?" snorted Siri. "I'll eat you, then I'll wash."

"I am surprised!" chirped the bird. "I would never have taken you for such a bad-mannered cat."

"Bad mannered!" growled Siri. "I'm a well-brought up pussy with impeccable manners! Didn't the Grand Vizier buy this house for me? Is not his wife now my slave with nothing to do but comb my hair and fill my bowl? And was not my mother a palace cat?"

"Ho! I can tell you a thing or two. Manners! Manners your mother must have forgotten to teach you," scoffed the bird. "I fly over the palace every day and there are the royal cats, every cat washing *before* it eats from its golden bowl."

Siri closed her eyes to slits and stared narrowly at the bird who scolded. "You should know better, Puss. Even farm cats wash, then eat. And I believe that alley cats do so as well."

Siri listened. She had nothing to say and the bird went on, "Even kittens know that it is the correct thing to do in polite society. I am astounded that you do *not* wash before you eat!"

"But I do," Siri told her huffily. "Yes, I do." And she sat up very straight and proudly displayed her chest, then lifting a paw, she delicately licked its pads with her pink, sand-papery tongue. *Lick!* She began to wash her face and the bird slipped from beneath the other paw, fluttered past her nose and flew up to a tree. "You shouldn't believe everything you hear, Puss!" the bird called down to her.

"Sssssspppt!" hissed Siri, realizing that she'd been tricked. And to this day no self-respecting cat washes until after a meal is eaten. And very clean animals they are.

> If a cat is seen washing
> it is a sign of good luck
> If a cat washes behind its
> ears then it will rain today.

CAT BATH

Sometimes a cat's busy tongue can't wash away stubborn mud, clay, car grease or paint which is soiling her fur. You can help by giving her a bath. Of course, the cat will hate it. They are not soap-and-water lovers. So you may need a grown-up or two to help shampoo the cat.

First of all, decide where to do the bathing. The laundry tub perhaps.

Now collect together some baby shampoo because a cat's skin is very tender. Two large towels for drying her fur. A heater if the day is cool. Never bath the cat on a cold day. You'll also need lots of luke-warm water. One lot for the shampooing and the other for rinsing. Add a little vinegar to the rinsing water to help with tangles if the cat's hair is long.

Now find the cat. If she's been bathed before she will have hidden.

Her claws could be trimmed in case of scratches but that is a job for a grown-up to do.

Dip the cat up to her neck in the water and work quickly. One person shampoos while someone else holds her firmly. Talk to her all the time. It will help to calm her and reassure her that she's not going to drown.

Dunk her quickly into the rinsing water.

Wrap her in towels and rub her fur as dry as you can. Now let her take over. She'll settle somewhere warm and then lick-lick-lick. Surprisingly this will not make her wetter. She'll soon look tidy and sleek again.

Don't bath the cat unless it's necessary.

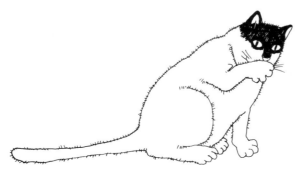

29

MOTHER SHUTTLE

Old Mother Shuttle
Lived in a coal-scuttle,
Along with her dog and her cat;
What they ate I can't tell
But it's known very well,
That not one of the party was fat.

Old Mother Shuttle
Scoured out her coal-scuttle,
And washed both her dog and her cat;
The cat scratched her nose,
So they came to hard blows,
And who was the gainer of that?

AT-CHOOM!

Three lit tle old men went to the woods. When they came out they

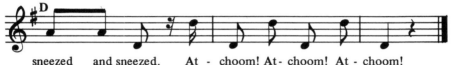

sneezed and sneezed. At - choom! At- choom! At - choom!

Three little fat lads	Three little lassies
Went to the woods.	Went to the woods.
When they came out	When they came out
They sneezed and sneezed.	They sneezed and sneezed.
A-choo! A-choo! A-choo!	*Tish-oo! Tish-oo! Tish-oo!*

Make the song your own. Sing and sneeze for anyone who may have nipped into the woods and caught cold.
How do you think a tiger would sneeze? Or a fox? An elephant? A butterfly? And have you heard a cat sneeze? Lucky is the bride who hears a cat sneeze. She will be happy for the rest of her life, so it is said in France where this song was first sung to children. It can also be sung as a Round. One person begins, others join in, one after the other, and the song goes round in a circle of music.

A PLACE BY THE FIRE

In the long ago days of Once-There-Was, Wild Tiger lived with Little Wild Cat. And they lived in a cave somewhere in the depths of the green-green jungle. Wild Tiger hunted and Little Wild Cat kept the cave clean. So that was a happy arrangement.

Achoo! Tishoooo! Wild Tiger came home one morning with a cold instead of something to eat. A-a-a-achoooo! A bad cold! A-*a-a-a*-choo! Wild Tiger shivered. He sniffled and shook with cold. His throat hurt. His ears were sore. His head ached. All of him ached as far down as his claws! Then he felt very hot. Next he was very cold. And he sneezed, and he sneezed.

"You have a fever," said Little Wild Cat. "Lie down inside the cave. I'll bring you some milk."

"I-I'm c-c-cold! So c-c-cold!" whispered Wild Tiger and his teeth cha-cha-chattered as if they were about to shake out of his gums. "My c-coat no longer w-warms m-me!"

"It is the fever," soothed Little Wild Cat. "I shall run to the village and bring back fire, the kind that men use there. It will warm you. Now, I shan't be long."

And so Little Wild Cat slipped from the cave. Like a shimmering shadow she passed along hidden cat-walks to the village, to tip-toe from hut to hut until she found one with a fire still burning on its hearth. As well as seeing the fire, Little Wild Cat smelt fish, and she smelt rice. She saw them then, both filling a bowl by the hearth.

Little Wild Cat helped herself to the food, emptying the bowl. Mmmm! It was better than Wild Tiger's offerings. Mmmmm! She felt pleasantly full and drowsy as she stretched herself long and thin and began to wash her face. "This is the way to live," she murmured. "I like it," she purred, and went to sleep.

Back in the cave, the cold and dark cave, Wild Tiger shivered and shook and sneezed, and grew more and more miserable while he waited for Little Wild Cat's return. He was so unhappy he opened his mouth and roared of his sorrow. His sad cry rolled out of the cave, down to the village and Little Wild Cat heard him through her sleep.

She opened her eyes and she stretched a little. She stood up, shook the sleep from her bones, scooped up a pawful of hot coals into a leaf and with a tiny yawn stepped from the hut. Then, she slipped out of the village and along the secret cat-ways to the cave. "Now you'll soon be warm," she told Wild Tiger as she kindled the fire. "There!" she purred when it began to burn cheerfully.

"I feel better already," smiled the tiger.

"I'm very glad to hear that," prinkled Little Wild Cat. "It is good news because I have decided that I will not be a wild jungle cat any longer. I am going to the village to live with man." And she trotted out of the cave with her tail in the air. "Goodbye!" she mewed sweetly.

"Come back!" roared Wild Tiger. "Come back, come back!"

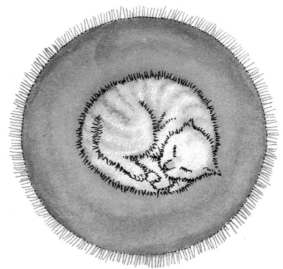

But Little Wild Cat ran quickly, quickly, quickly, back to the house with the fire.

She nosed in through the door, looked into the fish bowl in case she had left a morsel there uneaten, but as there was not a scrap she washed herself sleek and tidy, then curled into a circle by the fire.

And there she stayed. She forgot about the time when she had lived with Wild Tiger in the cold damp cave in the green-green jungle. And with time he forgot about her as well.

PUSSY WANTS A CORNER

This is an old game which can be played indoors, especially on wet days — if the adults don't mind too much noise and excitement. One or two of them may join in, if you are short of players. You need *five* people and *four* corners, and plenty of room to dash about without knocking over furniture.

Everyone gathers into the centre of the playing space. Count to three. All rush for a corner. The one who misses capturing a corner becomes Puss. Now Puss goes to each player in turn, mewing "Pussy wants a corner! Pussy wants a corner!" "Poor Pussy! Go to my neighbour!" each player tells Puss. When Puss has been refused by all four, there's nothing else to do but to pad sadly to the centre of the

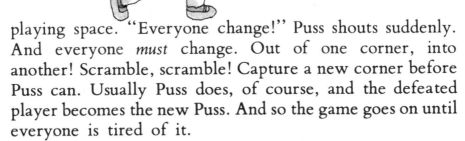

playing space. "Everyone change!" Puss shouts suddenly. And everyone *must* change. Out of one corner, into another! Scramble, scramble! Capture a new corner before Puss can. Usually Puss does, of course, and the defeated player becomes the new Puss. And so the game goes on until everyone is tired of it.

However, if at any time Puss misses a corner in the scramble the game still goes on as before.

Should more children want to play, then agree upon places to be extra corners. You should always have one corner less than the number of players.

CAT COMFORT

Cats are fussy. To help a long-haired cat to be well-groomed you will need a brush and comb for daily hair-dressing.

Cats are flea-haters. A flea collar may be appreciated by your cat.

Cats are clean. If your cat lives indoors it will need a litter box which can be a tray, or a cut-down carton. Line the box with shredded newspapers, sawdust, or clean dry sand. Empty it daily.

Cats are prowlers. Cats like to come and go, especially at night. A *chatiére*, a special cat-sized door can be cut into the human's door. No one then, is forced to hop out of bed to let the cat in or out.

Cats are stay-at-homes. Some cats will travel happily in a car if trained from kitten days, but most cats become scratching-frantic with fear and howl with terror. Beg, borrow or buy a cat basket with a secure lid if a cat is to be moved.
Some people butter a cat's paws to help calm the animal. It keeps Puss busily licking its paws clean.

Cats are comfort-lovers. Cats like their own cushion, or rug, or even personal chair. Sometimes a page from a newspaper can become a cat-mat.

CAT NAPS

Cats sleep where they're able —
Any cupboard, any table,
Top of bookshelf, on your lap,
Empty box, or a cosy gap
          near the fireplace.
On the bed, under your pillow
or a sunny spot beneath the willow,
In the sun or in the shade,
any space seems specially made
          — for Puss!

Margaret Hamilton

THE CAT'S PYJAMAS

The Cat's Pyjamas are not meant for a drowsy cat but for a person to keep pyjamas tidily in one place during the day. Very useful for pyjama losers! You may need some help to make it but do as much as you can.

From a firm, unpatterned material cut 2 circles each with a radius of 150 mm.

Sew the two circles together, leaving an opening as shown. Hem the edges of the opening. This is the cat's head.

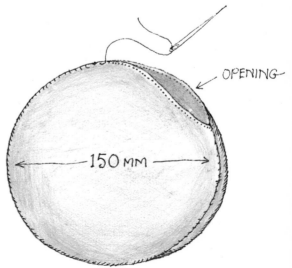

OPENING

150 MM

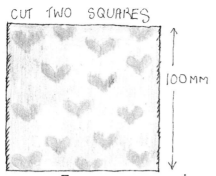

CUT TWO SQUARES

100MM

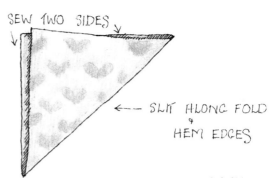

SEW TWO SIDES

←— SLIT ALONG FOLD
&
HEM EDGES

STITCH

OPENING

From a contrasting or patterned material cut two squares which measure about 100 mm on each side. These will become the ears.

To make the ears, fold each square into a triangle. Stitch two sides firmly, then slit along the fold. Hem the edges.

Fit each ear into position on the head, pin, then stitch. Use an embroidery stitch, such as cross-stitch if you like, or a contrasting coloured thread. Use a felt pen to draw on the cat's features, or embroider his features. Use scraps of material and sew on eyes, nose and mouth. Or use all three kinds of decoration. Don't forget the whiskers.

Fatten the cat's face with your pyjamas or nightgown. Press-studs can be used to clip the opening.

The cat-face also makes a cushion if filled with scraps of stuffing. Stitch the opening firmly. A cushion looks it best if the filling is placed inside a separate bag. Two circles of scrap material cut slightly smaller than the cat's face is all that's needed to make this. Leave an opening to push in the filling, then stitch it closed. Push the filling into the cat's face now. Stitch its opening closed. Shake the cushion to help the filling settle evenly.

←— PRESS STUDS

A CONVERSATION
IN THE MIDDLE OF THE NIGHT

"What's that?"
"Just the cat."
"Are you sure?"
"She's at the door."
"Then let her out!"
"Out, Cat!"
"Scat!"

PILLOWCASE CAT

An old Cat found that she could no longer hunt mice and so, she sat herself in the sun and wondered, "How can I entice the mice to run into my paws?"

The only way to deceive a mouse was to pretend that she was dead. "Aaaah! I'll hang myself upside-down from a peg on the door of the cupboard," she decided.

It was a difficult task she had set herself but she managed to carry out her plan with the help of a torn pillowcase.

Before long, one mouse, then two mice, three, four, five mice and more came from their holes to scamper about, close to the innocent-looking, dangling paws, but ... not quite close enough. "Keep your distance, my friends!" a wise old Gaffer-mouse whispered. "Many an old bag have I seen in my day, but, never one with a cat's head at the bottom of it," he warned.

Then the old Mouse turned to the very uncomfortable cat, "Hang there, good Madam, hang as long as you please, but I would not trust myself to come within reach of you, even if you were stuffed with straw."

And that was that!

41

BELLING THE CAT

Some other mice were forever attacked by another cat. The mice held a Council of War to decide what they could do with their fierce enemy. Brown Mouse said, "Let's form an army and declare war on the Cat. We'll drive him from the house."

"No, no!" said the others. "A mouse army would be no match for the Cat."

"Build a cage and bait it with a fish-head," suggested Grey Mouse. "The Cat will be lured in. We shut the door and lock it. The Cat would be freed only if he promised never again to attack us."

"No, no!" said the others. "It isn't possible for us to build a cage."

"Someone can creep up on the sleeping Cat and tie a bell to his neck," said Tan Mouse. "Then, whenever the bell tinkled we would know that the Cat was near. We'd have plenty of time to scurry to our holes."

The mice cheered. It was a wonderful idea! The cheering went on and on, then someone asked, "Who is to tie the bell to the Cat?"

No one answered. No one dared. And so ...

The Cat still attacks.

The Mice still run.

THE OLD GREY CAT

The old grey cat is sleep-ing, sleep-ing, sleep-ing, The

old grey cat is sleep-ing in the house

Verses 1, 3, 4, 6 play in G major.
Verses 2 and 5 play in G minor to dramatise creeping movement
Verse 6 increase tempo for mouse scamper

The little mice are creeping, creeping, creeping,
The little mice are creeping through the house.

The little mice are nibbling, nibbling, nibbling,
The little mice are nibbling in the house.

The little mice are sleeping, sleeping, sleeping,
The little mice are sleeping in the house.

The old grey cat is creeping, creeping, creeping,
The old grey cat is creeping through the house.

The little mice all scamper, scamper, scamper,
The little mice all scamper through the house.

Does the old grey cat catch the mice? It depends how you decide to play the game. Decide who will be the cat. Everyone else is a mouse. Do as the song tells, ending with a grand chase. If a mouse is caught, that mouse must change places with the cat, then the song and game begin again.

ROOSTER KING

Would you believe that a rooster was once the King of the
Cats? Indeed, he was! In Africa. In a certain village. And he
was a very bad king! He strutted round and round the
village, showing off his bright red comb and crowing loud
enough to be heard deep in the jungle. "I'm the King of the
Cats! Look at my fierce red comb, you cats! It is red with
fire. Disobey me and I'll burn every one of you!"

"Ourrrrr!" howled the cats. Not one wanted to be
burned. Not one wanted singed fur. Not only would it look
unsightly, but singed fur smells very bad.

"Bring me breakfast!" screamed Rooster. "Bring fresh
worms from the jungle." And the cats sprinted into the

44

dark, leafy jungle and scratched up the longest of worms for Rooster King.

"Fetch me lunch!" Rooster shrieked. "The fattest and ripest of grass-seeds! Be quick about it! Don't keep me waiting!" And the cats scattered to search for grass-seeds, which are difficult to harvest with paws.

"Catch me dinner!" screeched Rooster. "The flyingest flying ants of the choicest kind. Nothing else will do! Get moving, cats!" Rooster waggled his comb threateningly and the cats leaped and snatched at the flying ants, then dangling the insects by their wings from their mouths, they presented their king with his feast.

The Rooster grew fat. The cats grew thin. Rooster worked them like slaves. Every day was the same. The cats longed to prowl at night and snooze all day because that is the way of cats. They dared not. Rooster would burn holes in their fur.

Then, at last, there came the days of the Long Rains. It rained heavy soaking rain for days and days. It rained on the fires under the cats' cooking pots. *Pssst!* It snuffed out the fires. Every fire!

"Rooster King has fire in his comb," said Boss Cat. "Someone will have to go to him and ask for a little of his fire. Who will it be?"

No one wanted to go, of course. Then a kitten who was big enough to carry a message, felt very brave and he went, taking his best pussy-cat manners with him. "Oh, Great and Graciously Magnificent Majesty!" Kitten said very politely. "Oh, King! The rain has doused our cooking-pot fires. May we beg a little of the fire from your comb?"

Rooster didn't answer. He was asleep, perched on an old

stump which he used as his throne. When he didn't stir Kitten scampered back to his mother. "Rooster is asleep so I have no fire," he told her.

"Go back again, Kitlin," mewed his mother. "Take this dry grass. Hold it close to his comb. When it catches alight bring it back to me."

The Rooster was still sleeping when the kitten returned. He scrambled up the stump, holding the dried grass stalks in his teeth. "Your Majesty!" said the kitten. "May I take some fire from your comb?"

Again there was no answer. The kitten held the grass between two paws and placed it against the rooster's comb. Nothing happened. Kitten moved the grass to another position. Still the grass did not light. He fanned it with his breath. He blew and blew at it. Nothing! The grass would not catch alight.

So back to Mother Cat he went. "Tsk! Perhaps you didn't do exactly as I said," his mother mewed. "I'll go myself."

She found the Rooster sleeping and she held the grass to his comb. Nothing happened. She held the grass here, there, here again, everywhere. It did not catch alight. She fanned and she blew to encourage a tiny flame. Nothing! So she touched the comb with a paw. It was hardly warm! It felt strange, like an old banana skin. "It is only the colour of fire," murmured Mother Cat. "Wake up! Wake up, you

old fraud," she snarled. *Biff-bang!* She pushed the rooster. *Smick-smack! Squawk!* Rooster was knocked off his stump throne. "There is *no* fire in your comb. You are *no longer* the King of the Cats! Find your own meals in future!" she told him.

And that's how it has been in the barnyard ever since.

BARNYARD SONG

I had a cat, and the cat pleased me, I fed my cat by yon-der tree; Cat goes fid-dle-dee - dee. I had a hen and the hen pleased me, I fed my hen by yon - der

Repeat this section as needed

tree; Hen goes chim - my - chuck, chim - my - chuck, Cat goes fid - dle-dee - dee.

Fine

I had a duck and the duck pleased me,
I fed my duck by yonder tree;
Duck goes quack-quack, quack-quack,
Hen goes chimmy-chuck, chimmy-chuck,
Cat goes fiddle-dee-dee.

I had a pig and the pig pleased me,
I fed my pig by yonder tree;
Pig goes griffy-gruff, griffy-gruff,
Duck goes quack-quack, quack-quack,
Hen goes chimmy-chuck, chimmy-chuck,
Cat goes fiddle-dee-dee.

Keep on adding farm animals with their sounds to make the
song the biggest and noisiest of barnyards.

CLUCKY HEN

Clucky Hen is made from a small tin and string, paint and paper for decorations.

If the tin has sharp or ragged edges they should be flattened so that there is no danger of cut fingers. Next thing is to hammer a nail hole in the bottom of the tin. Someone is sure to do it for you, if you need help.

Paint the tin white. It's a good colour for a chook. Cut some red paper into a comb shape and a beak. Paste these into position. Make paper eyes too, if you like. Or draw these.

Trim the string to about 1 metre long. Thread it through the hole in the tin. Tie a knot in the end so it can't pull free. Rub some resin on the string. Now the hen is ready to cluck.

Dangle the tin-hen by its string. With the other hand jerk and twang the string with your fingers and thumb.

Cluck-cluck-cluck! croons your hen.

NINE LIVES

My kitty-cat has nine lives,
Yes, nine long lives has she —
Three to spend in eating,
Three to spend in sleeping,
And three to spend in the chestnut tree.

DO I HAVE NINE LIVES TOO?

THE CAT'S DINNER

Cats shouldn't eat ice-cream. It's food for children. However, cats are natural hunters and they like to eat a variety of things.

Your cat may like fish, raw eggs, chicken, meat, rabbit, tinned cat food, vegetables, milk and small amounts of kidney and liver.

Feed your cat in the same place each day. Be sure that the cat's bowl is as clean as your own dishes and watch her drinking bowl. It should always hold fresh clean water.

Kittens should be fed four times each day until about 12 weeks old. An egg yolk beaten into one cup of the kitten's milk will help it to grow into a strong cat.

ANYTHING FOR FISH

Furbelow, handsome and elegant as any prince of cats, had manners fit for the dust-bin. When the cook at his house prepared fish for dinner he twisted and wove about her legs, begging and mewing, until she stamped her feet with annoyance. Then, as soon as her back was turned, Furbelow sprang up to the bench to steal fish. Cook rapped his nose smartly. All Furbelow ended up with was the delicious fishy smell which was so delightful it nearly drove him mad. He'd do anything for a piece of fish!

When it was carried to the table, Furbelow went too, escorting the dish. And while his master ate, Furbelow lovingly stared up at him, mewing little purring love-songs, or tapping his master's knee to remind him of his need of a fish dinner as well. All Furbelow received for his efforts were the bones and the tail.

Then, oh, then! Furbelow discovered that fish lived in the lagoon which was beyond the house. Alas, the fish lived under the water and Furbelow loathed wet feet, yet he refused to be dismayed. He crouched on the edge of the bank watching the fish gliding by, so close to his nose. "Fish, little fish!" he shouted down to them. "Your lagoon is to be drained. What will you do when the last drop of water has gone?"

That caused a stir, I can tell you. The fish flipped and flapped until the water seemed to be boiling. They called a meeting at once. What was to be done? They would die if the lagoon were drained. Would the pussy-cat carry them away to the safety of the sea? The fish sent a crab to ask the cat.

"Yes, I'll help the fish," answered Furbelow. "Tell them I can carry only one fish at a time. Let a fish jump to the bank and I'll run with it to the sea. Then, I'll come back for the next fish."

No time was lost. The first fish flipped out of the water. Furbelow picked it up in his mouth and ran off, up over a sand-dune and out of sight. Then he was back again. Another fish flipped from the water, and away went Furbelow once more.

So it went on. Furbelow rescued fish. Then, Crab sidled up to the cat. "Please, I don't think I can walk as far as the sea," said Crab. "Would you, dear Pussy, carry me there? I don't want to be left behind when the lagoon is drained."

"All right!" said Furbelow. "I've taken a fancy to you. Before I carry another fish, I'll take you." And Furbelow took Crab up by one claw and hurried off, up over the sand-dune and into the spikey grass.

"This isn't the way to the sea," thought Crab, although he could smell a fishy smell. The smell grew stronger. It was far from fresh. Then, Crab saw the bones strewn amongst the grass. Delicate, lacy, foam-white fishbones! "Well I'm not going to be the cat's next meal," thought Crab. He swung up his free claw. He nipped Furbelow's nose.

Miaowwwww! Furbelow screeched and leapt high.

Crab was thrown into the air and he clutched out with the other claw. He nipped Furbelow's ear and Furbelow danced with pain.

Crab dropped down to the sand and with a sideways lurch scuttled off, back to the lagoon.

Furbelow went home, and, if he ever went by the lagoon again he sprinted past with his nose in the air and never a glance for anywhere but straight ahead. He still ate fish however, when he could persuade his family to share theirs.

SERVES HIM RIGHT!

HERE IS THE SEA
A finger game

Here is the sea, the wavy sea.
Here is the boat and here is me.

Use one hand to make wave movements
Hold the other hand in a fist over the waves.
It's the boat. Pop up the thumb to be "me".

And the little fishes down below
Wiggle their tails and away they go.

Stop making waves and wiggle fingers as the fish under the
boat.
Gliding and swerving, swim the fish-fingers away.

Who teaches her young to snatch and grab?
None other than nippity Mumma Crab.

FAT CAT

On a farm in Denmark there once lived a Farmer and his Goody Wife, and their Very Greedy Fat Cat. The cat ate so much that the Farmer and his wife could no longer afford to keep her. "You must find a home of your own, Puss," the Goody said as she filled the cat's bowl with cream.

The Very Greedy Fat Cat lapped up the cream and then, believe it or not, she ate up the Goody, herself. She *did!*

Then, jumping out of the window she ran to the field where the Husband was working. "Good day, Puss!" said he. "Have you eaten your cream?"

"I have. And I've eaten the little old Goody," said the Very Greedy Fat Cat. "I still feel hungry so I'm going to eat you too." And believe it or not, she ate up the little old Husband.

After that, the Very Greedy Fat Cat licked her chops, washed her face and toddled to the dairy where the Blossy Cow waited to be milked. "Good day, Puss!" mooed Blossy. "Have you eaten your cream?"

"I have. And I have eaten the little old Goody and her little old Husband," said the Very Greedy Fat Cat. "I still feel hungry so I'm going to eat you too." And believe it or not, she ate up Blossy Cow, horns, hoofs and all the rest.

Hey-ho! The Very Greedy Fat Cat ran into the forest. Who did she meet but Reynard Fox and he barked, "Good day, Puss! Have you eaten your cream?"

"I have. And I've eaten the little old Goody, her little old Husband and Blossy Cow," said the Very Greedy Fat Cat. "I still feel hungry so I'm going to eat you too." And believe it or not, she ate up Reynard Fox, including his long brush tail.

And away she padded, deeper into the forest. Oh-oh! Along loped Greylegs Wolf! "Good day, Puss!" he growled. "Have you eaten your cream?"

"I have. And I have eaten the little old Goody, her little old Husband, Blossy Cow and Reynard Fox," said the Very Greedy Fat Cat. "I still feel hungry so I'm going to eat you too." And believe it or not, she ate up Greylegs Wolf, including his ears.

Ho-ho! Deeper and deeper into the forest she rambled, to the very feet of Brawny Bear, a cub no taller than you. "Good day, Puss!" rumbled Brawny. "Have you eaten your cream?"

"I have. And I have eaten the little old Goody, her little old Husband, Blossy Cow, Reynard Fox and Greylegs Wolf," said the Very Greedy Fat Cat. "I still feel hungry so I'm going to eat you too." And . . . yes, she ate up Brawny Bear Cub.

Mother Bear shambled up looking for her cub just as the Very Greedy Fat Cat closed her mouth. "Good day, Puss!" growled Mother Bear. "Have you eaten your cream?"

"I have. And I have eaten the little old Goody, her little
old Husband, Blossy Cow, Reynard Fox, Greylegs Wolf
and Brawny Bear Cub," said the Very Greedy Fat Cat. "I
still feel hungry so I'm going to eat you too." And she *did!*

Then she waddled to the edge of the forest, the other
side, mind you. Crossing her path lumbered Father Bear,
searching for his family. "Good day, Puss!" he rumbled.
"Have you eaten your cream?"

"I have. And I have eaten the little old Goody, her little
old Husband, Blossy Cow, Reynard Fox, Greylegs Wolf,
Brawny Bear Cub and Mother Bear," said the Very Greedy
Fat Cat. "I still feel hungry so I'm going to eat you too."
She did!

Well now, the Very Greedy Fat Cat zig-zagged, then zig-zagged out of the forest, into a village, just as a bridal party was leaving the church after an orange-blossom wedding. "Good day, Puss!" called the Bridegroom. "Have you eaten your cream?"

"I have. And I have eaten the little old Goody, her little old Husband, Blossy Cow, Reynard Fox, Greylegs Wolf, Brawny Bear Cub, Mother Bear and Father Bear," said the Very Greedy Fat Cat. "I still feel hungry so I'm going to eat you too." And ... wait for it! She ate up the Bridegroom-and-his-Bride, the-Groomsmen-and-the-Bridesmaids, the-Parson, the-Piper, the-Cake-maker-and *all* the-Wedding-guests.

The Very Greedy Fat Cat staggered along the road to meet a funeral party on its way to the cemetery. The Undertaker took off his hat. "Good day, Puss!" he droned. "Have you eaten your cream?"

"I have. And I have eaten the little old Goody, her little old Husband, Blossy Cow, Reynard Fox, Greylegs Wolf, Brawny Bear Cub. Mother Bear, Father Bear, the Bridegroom-and-his-Bride, the-Groomsmen-and-the-Bridesmaids, the-Parson, the-Piper, the-Cake-maker-and *all* the-Wedding-guests," said the Very Greedy Fat Cat. "I still feel hungry so I'm going to eat you too." And I hope you've been keeping count of all of these people because the Very Greedy Fat Cat, not only ate up the Undertaker *but* the Pall Bearers, the Man-in-the-Coffin, and all the Mourners, and goodness only knows how many there were of them!

Phew! The Very Greedy Fat Cat was unable to move. It won't surprise you at all to know that she just sat in the middle of the road. She began to clean her whiskers and a mouse peeked from a bush. "Hi, Cat!" it shrilled and shook an ear of wheat under the Very Greedy Fat Cat's nose. "Are you hungry?" shouted Mouse. It skipped up and down in front of the Very Greedy Fat Cat. "Tee-hee-hee! Bet you can't catch me, Cat!"

O-oh! The Very Greedy Fat Cat's eyes glittered through pencil slits of lowered lids. She tensed. She sprang at the bouncing Mouse. She landed . . . on nothing, except her four paws, and then, before you could smile, the Very Greedy Fat Cat exploded. *Pop-p-p!* It was as if she'd been pricked by a pin.

Out stepped the little Old Goody, her little old Husband, Blossy Cow, Reynard Fox, Greylegs Wolf, Brawny Bear Cub, Mother Bear, Father Bear, the Bridegroom-and-his-Bride, the-Groomsmen-and-the-Bridesmaids, the-Parson, the-Piper, the-Cake-maker-and *all* the-Wedding-guests, the Undertaker and the Pall Bearers, the Man-in-the-Coffin and all the Mourners, and goodness only knows how many there were of them. Each one was as good as new, including the Man-in-the-Coffin who was now alive and kicking and screaming to be let out. That was attended to at once.

And that was the end of that, particularly the Very Greedy Fat Cat and you can believe it or not, just as *you* please.

I KNOW AN OLD LADY

I know an old la-dy who swall-owed a fly,

I don't know why she swall-owed a fly.

I guess she'll die. I know an old la-dy who

swall-owed a spi-der that wrig-gled and jig-gled and

tick-led in-side her; She swall-owed the spi-der to

catch the fly. I don't know why she

swall owed a fly. I guess she'll die.

I know an old lady who swallowed a bird,
How absurd to swallow a bird!
She swallowed the bird to catch the spider
That wriggled and jiggled and tickled inside her,
She swallowed the spider to catch the fly,
I don't know why she swallowed a fly.
I guess she'll die.

I know an old lady who swallowed a cat,
Imagine that! She swallowed a cat!
She swallowed the cat to catch the bird,
She swallowed the bird to catch the spider
That wriggled and jiggled and tickled inside her,
She swallowed the spider to catch the fly,
I don't know why she swallowed a fly.
I guess she'll die.

I know an old lady who swallowed a dog,
What a hog to swallow a dog!
She swallowed the dog to catch the cat, etc.

I know an old lady who swallowed a goat,
Opened her throat and swallowed a goat!
She swallowed the goat to catch the dog, etc.

I know an old lady who swallowed a cow,
I don't know how she swallowed a cow!
She swallowed a cow to catch a goat, etc.

I know an old lady who swallowed a horse,
(SPOKEN) She's dead, of course!

DEVIL-MOUSE

When Noah built the ark he took on board a pair of every living creature that lived thereabouts. Two by two, the animals and the birds and the fish climbed into the ark. Then Noah's two sons and their wives entered the ark. Last of all came Noah and his wife.

Now, some people say that as Noah shut the door he snapped off the tail of a cat who arrived late, dangling a mouse from her jaws, if you please. Certainly tailless cats live on the Isle of Man to this day. Whether this was so, or not, Noah seemed to have cat-trouble, one way and another. And who was at the bottom of it all? A mouse! An extra mouse, a third mouse which should not have been on board the ark at all! It had nipped in when no one was looking.

But then that mouse was not an ordinary mouse of the kind that you and I have seen. Noah either, for that matter. It was a devil-mouse. A wicked little devil disguised as a mouse! Just as well they are no longer about because the devil-mouse was plump and furry like any other little grey mouse. And he had pink paws, a sharp little nose, a long tail and bright eyes as small as a pearl of sago. Those eyes quickly spied a good dark hiding place in a corner of the ark.

Outside it was raining. It rained and it rained. It rained for forty days and forty nights, flooding the countryside in a sea of water which picked up the ark and floated it away.

While the ark sailed across the flood-sea that wicked little devil-mouse was hard at work chewing at a plank in the ark's hull. "I'll chew a big hole and sink this ark," it told itself as it gnawed and gnawed. "Water will pour through my hole and Noah and his lot will drown," it mumbled through a mouthful of wood.

Around the hole a pile of wood shavings was growing. The wicked little devil-mouse kicked some out of its way and began gnawing once more.

Noah saw the wood-dust when he came to fetch a fresh bag of grain for the animals' porridge. "What's this?" he asked. "What's this?" He peered into the corner. He saw the hole. He saw the mouse. "What are you doing?" he shouted at the wicked, little devil-mouse and Noah threw his glove at it.

Plop! The glove fell over the mouse and ... and-and-and it turned into a cat! The palm and the back of the glove became the cat's body and head. The four fingers changed to four long legs and the thumb swished angrily as a tail.

The cat caught the mouse by its neck, gave it a shake and a nip with sharp teeth, and that was the end of the wicked little devil-mouse.

And it was almost the end of the cat. She had broken the peace on board the ark. Until then, the lamb had fed with the wolf, the lion had slept by the deer, the fox had drunk with the rabbit. No animal feared any other.

"Cat, by the grace of God you have saved the ark from sinking into the flood," Noah said. "Alas, to do so, you have killed. I cannot let you stay on board the ark."

Noah sadly took the cat into his arms. She was still holding the mouse when he threw them both into the waters.

At once the cat swam back to the ark's doorstep to pull herself up to it. Settling comfortably she licked her wet fur into place. Cat then stretched out lazily in the sunshine.

Ever since that day, her children and their children and all cats ever after have chased mice, and cats will swim only if need be. No cat likes wet fur, or wet paws. All cats like a doorstep and other warm spots for dozing in the sun.

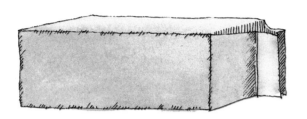

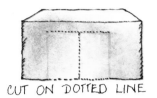

CUT ON DOTTED LINE

NOAH'S ARK

You can make an ark. Find an empty milk carton to make the hull. Give it a good wash to keep it smelling sweetly.

Lay the carton on its side.

Find a smaller box about the size that holds wirewool for the kitchen. This will be the cabin. Make a door in one side by carefully cutting as we've shown. Bend the pieces back as doors opening and closing. Glue the box to the carton-hull, or fasten it with sticky tape.

A piece of corrugated cardboard can rest on the top as a roof. Or bend the cardboard into a peaked roof. Fasten it with sticky tape.

The ark is ready for Noah, his family and the animals.

Make them from modelling clay, craft clay or salt and flour clay. String, cottonwool, beads, cotton, fringing, pipe cleaners and other odds and ends can be used to complete the figures. Paper or material scraps can be used for clothes. Another finish is to paint the models.

WHERE'S YOUR TAIL, PUSSY?

Pret, the cat, took it into his head that he wanted to travel. Now, Pret lived on an island, he did. The Isle of Man it was. The hills were pink with heather and the gorse ran golden down to the sea and the gulls shouted to each other above the cliff, or shrieked at the seals which sunned themselves on the rocks below. A pretty place it was but as Pret said, "A cat doesn't see much of the world if he stays in the one place all the time."

The farm cats yawned to hear this again and you'd be more interested than they were. "And I'm hearing that cats are wearing tails nowadays in Ramsey," said Pret. "Tails, if you please! I've never had a tail, nor my mother before me, or her mother before that! Whatever will cats be doing next, I ask you? I'd better be getting along to Ramsey, I'm thinking. I'll travel and take a look at these cats."

And Pret set off that morning to travel the road all day without one morsel to eat. By sundown he was grumbling, "It's hungry, I am. And tired, I am. I'll be seeing if the farmer people over there will be giving me a drop of milk."

As bold as brass Pret went stepping into the farmhouse

kitchen while the farmer's dog went berserk on the end of his chain to see Pret pass. "Will you be giving me some cream?" Pret asked.

"Will you be catching some rats then in the barn?" asked the farmer.

Pret stuck his nose in the air. "Hunting is for my own pleasure. I am *not* a working animal at all. I am a travelling cat, travelling for my education and to see the world. Get a common tabby to catch your rats, Sir."

"Ho-ho! You are a one for giving yourself airs," said the farmer. "No rats caught, then no cream, cat."

"Would you be giving me cream if I sing a song for it? I'm middling good at singing," preened Pret, and he began a caterwauling that would hurt your ears it was so awful to hear.

"I'll give you cream to stop that singing," yelled the farmer. And Pret soon had cream inside him. Then, what does he do but sit himself down on the hearth and say to the farmer's wife, "It's not here on the floor for me usually, but a soft cushion, or a feather bed under me. Cats like me are well looked upon where I come from, you know."

"You don't say!" said the wife, "and here was I believing that the very best cats all had long tails. Where's your tail, Pussy? Did I hear correctly that your family all lost theirs when Noah slammed the door on your ancestor. She'd stayed out late a-mousing, I heard."

"That's no more than an old tale," yawned Pret. "The first of our family roamed here from Egypt. Royal cats we were with a place on the steps to the king's own throne, but travelling is in our blood. That's why I'm here now."

Pret stretched his claws then drew them back into his pads as he purred down his long nose. "I'll be making an early start in the morning, so I'll be saying good-night to you now. You can put a bit of breakfast by me here, then I won't have to disturb you from your bed." Pret shut his green eyes then, and there wasn't another sound from him.

Away he went early in the morning. His rump up high and his front down low. "Where would you be going?" he greeted the farm dog. "Fetchin' in the cows now," barked the dog. "And you'd be going off to work, too?"

"Only ignorant bodies like yourself must work, not the likes of me," Pret called and ducked into a hedge where he couldn't be chased by the insulted dog.

Pret pattered into Castletown. Cats sat in windows. Cats sat on doorsteps. Cats sat on stone walls. Cats sat on garden lawns. And every cat had a tail! Tails like brushes! Tails like pokers! Tails tipped with white fur! Tails ringed with stripes! Tails! Very posh tails which they swished as they looked up at the sky to see which way the wind was blowing! Not a glance was spared for Pret! Not a sideways, side-long look! "Impudent felines!" mewed Pret. "None of them had a Great-great-great-gran from Egypt! And if it's their tails that they're so proud about, I'll show 'em a tail that'll set them lookin' and starin'. I will, I will!"

THERE ARE TOO MANY CATS ON THIS PAGE!

Pret ran himself to the butcher's to borrow a lamb's tail. And up, then down, the streets of Castletown he paraded with the lamb's tail stuck to his seat.

The town cats hooted and shrieked with laughter. Hoity-toity lot! Pret's whiskers twitched. He would show them. He would, he would!

He stalked by them all and took himself to Government House. "I've come to see the Governor's Lady," he told the guard. And Pret sat down on the place where his tail may have grown if he'd had one, and so the guard wasn't to know if he did have a tail or not. The guard said, "The Lady is taking tea with her cat from Siam and her cat from Persia."

"Then I've come to the right place. My Great-great-great-gran came from Egypt," purred Pret. "My ancestors sat on the steps of the king's throne." He gathered himself up and with a stately hippity-hop went to meet the Lady. "May you never be without herrings in your house!" Pret greeted her with a charming purr.

"Thank you!" answered the Lady with the grace of a princess. "What has brought you here, Pussikin?"

"I'm travelling for my education," Pret told her.

"Then let me give you a bowl of cream," she offered, and it was into three bowls she poured the cream, she did. A bowl full for each of her own cats and one for her guest. Pret lapped daintily, then wiped his mouth with a paw to

show that he was properly brought up. "I'll sing to you now," he announced. "I'm middling good at it."

He sat tall and straight and displayed his silken chest-fur, then started up such a caterwauling that the Siamese and the Persian couldn't resist joining in such a lovely song. And they all liked the sound of their voices mingling in harmony.

However, by the ninth chorus and as many verses the Governor's Lady couldn't stand to hear another note. "Ssssh!" she hushed them, "You'll be disturbing the Governor at his law-making."

An obliging cat was Pret. He lowered his voice to a purr-rumble and he lowered himself down on the rug by the fire. He folded his paws and fluffed his fur but he was too hot. So Pret stretched out long and lanky with every hair folded back into place against his skin. *Aaaah!* This was the life for a cat! And pretty soon Pret was asleep.

He woke and found himself in his own house, in his own place by the hearth, in the exact spot from where his travels began. Yes, he was home, he was!

The other cats said, "You've been a-dreamin', Pret." And never a word did they believe of his adventure! Pret went on boasting of it, even so. He talked about the time he sang to the Governor's Lady, and how a tail has nothing whatsoever to do with how well a cat can sing. One day those impudent cats of Castletown would discover that for themselves. As soon as they were educated, that is. They'd never shout then, "Where's your tail, Pussy?" They'd know what was what, just as did Pret, the wise and gracious one.

TAILS

Cows' tails go swishing round,
Cats' tails are twirly,
Wasps' tails have sharp stings,
Lambs' tails are bitty things
 and pigs' tails are curly.
Elephants' tails are thin like string,
Monkeys' tails are long and swing,
Snails' tails are little tails
leaving behind long silver trails.

NANCY'S CAT

Rat-a-tat-tat!

Now who in all the world was knocking at Nancy's door.
Who? And there it was, outside in the night, as black as
pitch. "I suppose it's someone wanting advice about a sick
cow," Nancy told herself. "Or it could be someone with a
sad love affair and wanting a bit of advice," she said as she
opened the door. And in stepped a great big black cat. And
he was as black as the night itself. Not a bit of white fur on
him at all! He walked himself up to Nancy and looked at
her with eyes as green as leaves on a tatie plant, and he said
as if he were singing a song, "Good evening to you Nancy!
I've come for a wee space by your fire."

"Well, *well!*" chortled Nancy. "Here's a cat talking like
a person, and even knowing the name Mother gave to me."

"And why shouldn't I be speaking to you now?" asked
the black cat. "Have I not lived for fifteen years with men
and women? I have as much right to talk as you yourself,
Nancy, me pretty. And I've a right to a full stomach too.
Will you be bringing me some cream then?"

"Will you listen to it! Ordering me about now!" chuckled Nancy.

"I'm tellin' you, me lovely, that the sides of me fur are nearly meeting. And while you get the cream you can be telling me why your hearth is empty? Are you not needing a cat now, Nancy?"

"No more cats for me," Nancy told him. "My old Tom died. If cats stay at home they die on you. If they go outdoors they don't come back, and a body's heart gets broken either way."

"I'll not be dying on you, and if I go outdoors it will be to bring you back a present of a fresh rabbit for our cooking pot," said the black cat. "That is a good enough reason for you to keep me, Nancy."

"But you are the wrong colour," Nancy told him. "My puss-cats have always been grey."

"And what's wrong with black?" bristled the big cat. "A black cat is esteemed by many. Besides, I could help you with your business."

"Then you win," said Nancy. "Make yourself at home and be welcomed."

And after that who had the warmest place by the hearth? Who had the softest down cushion? The feather pillow on the bed? The creamiest milk? The freshest fish? The big black cat, to be sure! And never another word did he speak! Never opened his mouth again, except to miaow. So what do you think of that?

Well now, the days brightened out of winter into spring and tufts of glossy black hair shed from the cat's fur, and a right mess he made of Nancy's house. It stuck to the pillows, the bed cover, Nancy's shawl and her mat on the floor.

"Pick up the hair, Nancy," ordered the black cat with the first words he had spoken for months. "Pick up that fur and spin it into yarn."

"And why would you be wanting yarn now?" asked Nancy.

"To knit into next winter's stockings for the Little Folk," black cat told her. "Fairies always wear stockings made from pussy-cat fur, don't you know?"

"I've never heard of such a thing in all my life!" said Nancy, but she set to spinning the hair into glossy thread which was as strong as silk.

"Now fetch me four knitting needles," said black cat.

"Listen to him now, ordering me about!" chortled Nancy. "In all me born days I've never seen a knitting cat!"

And a fine knitter he was. If you'd been there you would have seen how skilful he was with the needles and cat-yarn. *Click! click! Knit-knit!* Needles flashed. Stitches slipped and twisted. In no time a pair of stockings were made and they were no longer than a pussy-cat's tail. Think of that!

All through the summer the black cat knitted. Then he became restless. He had finished the yarn and had counted the stockings into pairs. He went prowling round the room, stepping to the window, going to the door, then the hearth, back to Nancy's chair, then back to the door. He could not settle. Nancy left him one night, pacing backwards and forwards, and went to bed.

Perhaps she slept for a little time before the hubbub started and set her sitting bolt upright in her bed. Up she hopped and crept to the bedroom door to see a crowd of little people trooping in from the moonlight, into her house, through the wide-opened door. They crowded round the black cat, touching him and shrieking delight in pop-corn voices. And as for that big black cat, he capered amongst them with the bag of stockings bouncing on his back.

Whhhhhhist! Out the door they danced to melt away in the moonbeams. Nancy stared after them. All was still now. The moonlight flooding in through the door glinted across the floor, to the table-top and over a saucer piled with gold coins.

"Look at that now!" breathed Nancy. "The black cat has paid for his board and keep, and my work on the stockings! Now what do you think of that?"

And what do *you* think?

Nancy bit a coin and knew it was gold, so she never wanted for anything as long as she lived. That's how much gold was in her gift. And, needless to say, she never saw the black cat again. And the next cat to sit on her hearth was grey, just as the other cats had been.

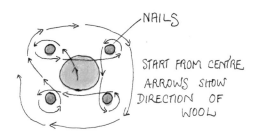

NAILS

START FROM CENTRE
ARROWS SHOW
DIRECTION OF
WOOL

KNITTING NANCY

Knitting Nancy is an old toy. Sometimes Nancy was made like a stout wooden doll with a painted face. You can make your own, perhaps with some help.

You start with a fat wooden cotton-reel, or a spool of some kind. Paint it if you like. Maybe give it a face with round red cheeks and wide-awake eyes.

Next, hammer four skinny nails as close as possible to the hole on one end of the reel. Space the nails evenly using those which have very small heads.

Find some scraps of wool, not too thick because it won't pull through the cotton-reel.

Thread the wool through the hole from the nailed end and allow a long end to dangle like a tail.

Hold Nancy in one hand to anchor the tail-dangle. With the other hand loop the wool about *each* nail, working the same way as the hands on a clock move. You have four stitches.

Now wind the wool about the outside of the stitches.

Find a fine knitting needle, or a thinly pointed stick and begin to knit. Using the knitting needle lift the first looped stitch over the wool on the outside of the nails. Go on to the next stitch, then the next, and the next.

Give the tail-dangle a little tug to pull the first row of stitches through the hole.

Keep on winding the wool about the nails, then lifting each loop in turn.

If you keep at it you'll make a long tube of knitting. It can be made into mats, teddy bear's ties, a trim for jumpers and other clothes, and whatever you can invent.

79

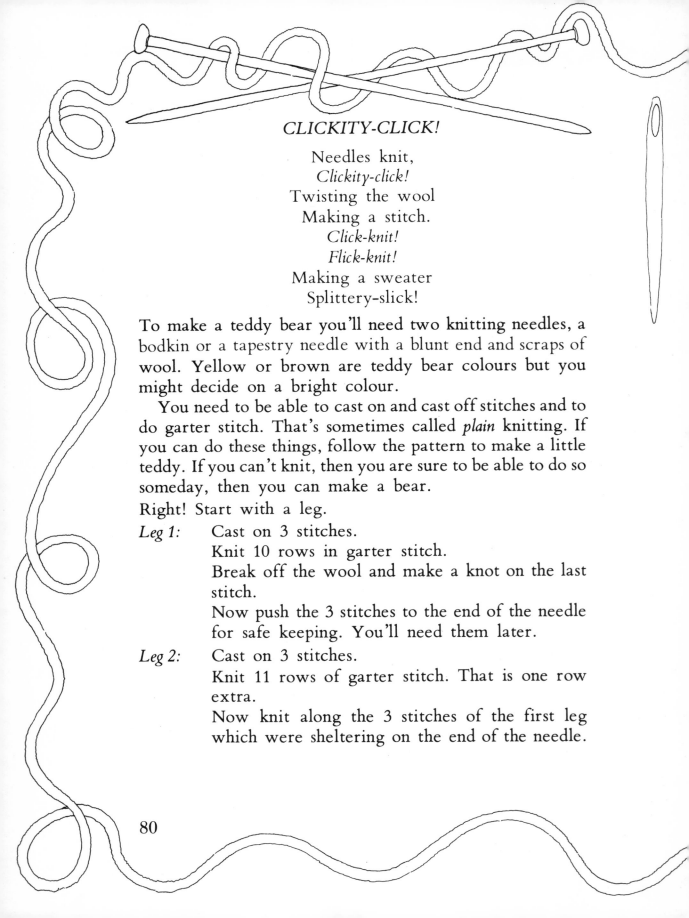

CLICKITY-CLICK!

Needles knit,
Clickity-click!
Twisting the wool
Making a stitch.
Click-knit!
Flick-knit!
Making a sweater
Splittery-slick!

To make a teddy bear you'll need two knitting needles, a bodkin or a tapestry needle with a blunt end and scraps of wool. Yellow or brown are teddy bear colours but you might decide on a bright colour.

You need to be able to cast on and cast off stitches and to do garter stitch. That's sometimes called *plain* knitting. If you can do these things, follow the pattern to make a little teddy. If you can't knit, then you are sure to be able to do so someday, then you can make a bear.

Right! Start with a leg.

Leg 1:   Cast on 3 stitches.

Knit 10 rows in garter stitch.

Break off the wool and make a knot on the last stitch.

Now push the 3 stitches to the end of the needle for safe keeping. You'll need them later.

Leg 2:   Cast on 3 stitches.

Knit 11 rows of garter stitch. That is one row extra.

Now knit along the 3 stitches of the first leg which were sheltering on the end of the needle.

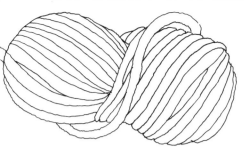

You now have 2 legs and 6 stitches.

Body: To make the teddy's body, cast on 1 stitch at the beginning of the next row.
Knit in garter stitch across the row of 7 stitches.
Cast on 1 stitch at the beginning of the next row.
That makes 8 stitches altogether now.
Knit 10 rows of garter stitch on the 8 stitches.
And now you're ready to make the arms.

Arms: Cast *on* 4 stitches at the beginning of the next row.
Cast *on* 4 stitches at the beginning of the next row.
Have you 16 stitches? You should have.
Cast *off* 4 stitches at the beginning of the next row.
Cast *off* 4 stitches at the beginning of the next row.
Ted now has two arms and you have 8 stitches again.

Neck and Head: Knit together 2 stitches at the beginning of the next row. Knit together 2 stitches at the end of the row. 6 stitches are left? Right!
Knit 2 rows of garter stitch.
Cast on 1 stitch at the beginning of the row. Cast on 1 stitch at the end of the row. 8 stitches again! They will make the bear's head.
Knit 8 rows of garter stitch.
Cast off.
Now, start from the beginning and knit another piece exactly the same.

Match the 2 pieces together and sew along the edges. Use an oversewing stitch and wool which is the same colour as the knitting. A tapestry needle or bodkin is best for this job. Leave the top of the bear's head open. Fill him with cotton-wool or scraps of shredded foam until he is fat and chubby. Stitch across the opening. Pull and push the corners into ear shapes. Embroider eyes and nose to his face. Tie a ribbon or a scrap of wool about his neck as a bow-tie. And one bear is finished. Why not make The Three Bears? The same pattern can be used but use differently sized needles and wools to suit. The thicker the wool, the fatter the needles should be and of course, you'll make a bigger bear.

When you are an expert bear knitter find a way to make other animals or dolls. A cat only needs long legs and a longer body. And a tail!

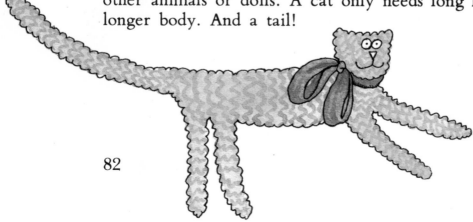

SWISH GOES THE BROOMSTICK!

There was an old witch,
Believe it if you can,
She tapped at the window
And she ran-ran-ran.
She ran helter-skelter,
With her toes in the air,
Cornstalks flying
From her old witchy hair.

Swish! goes her broomstick,
Meow! goes her cat,
Plop! goes her hop-toad
Sitting on her hat.
"Wee!" chuckled she,
"Hi-dee-ho-hi!
Hallowe'en night
When witches fly!"

VELVET PAWS

Once, in the old days of witches and spells there was a little witch, not much bigger than you. Even so, she was old, much older than one hundred years. And she was a bumble-footed, butter-fingered little witch. Forever dropping things and breaking things and making spells which didn't work and infuriating the other witches because she kept pet rabbits instead of slimy toads. Worse still, she called her cat Velvet Paws — an unheard of name! Everyone knows that a witch's cat should be called Grimalkin, or Holt, or Guzzle-Greedyguts, or even Pyewacket. Scream-in-the-Night was an acceptable name too, but Velvet Paws! She was not even a big black cat with eyes as green as pond weed like the hard-working cats that belonged to serious and proper witches. No! Velvet Paws was white from ear-tips to tail-tip. Her eyes were that sweet clear blue that you sometimes glimpse in a soap bubble at bathtime. She was a pretty little cat.

And there she was one morning, clinging desperately by her claws to the end of the Little Old Witch's broomstick as they flew above the forest trees. The Little Old Witch wasn't a good broomstick driver either and the other witches always tried to avoid her air-space. She dithered about, trying to decide whether to fly fast or slow, then she dipped and soared and did some fancy figure-eights which were more like lopsided sixes. Next came a loop-the-loop that was far too fast and I can tell you that Velvet Paws was feeling a little broomsick when ... *Banggggg!* The Little Old Witch had skimmed headfirst into a tree. She tumbled off the broom, flopped to the ground and lay there absolutely senseless.

Birds sang and insects buzzed. The breeze bustled and fussed in the leaves while the sun shone through the branches to glint gold between swaying shadows while the Little Old Witch lay as still as a rock with her broomstick poking down from a branch above her head.

She should *not* have been flying at that hour of the day. Serious witches always travel by the light of the moon, but then, the Little Old Witch wasn't clever with her spells and a failure with magic. It would be a long time before she was missed by the hard-working and skilled witches. So she lay there for five minutes, ten minutes, who knows how long?

Then, all at once, the forest became silent. The birds stopped singing and the insects stopped buzzing. The wind moved quietly now in the trees. *Sssssh!* Was that the wind then? Or was it something slipping through the long grass? *Sssssssh!*

A long, scaly, slithery snake glittered and slithered

85

towards the Little Old Witch. It flicked its tongue and hissed, "I can sssssswalllllow her in one gulp!"

Up and up he stretched. He hovered over the Little Old Witch, swaying and hissing, ready to strike.

Then . . . *spit-spat-ssscratch!* A ball of fur dropped from the tree to the snake's back. Claws dug deeply into the snake's skin. Needle-sharp teeth bit into flesh.

The snake writhed. It twisted and jerked into a spiral, striking out wildly with its tail, thrashing about with its head. It danced and looped in rage and pain but it could not throw off the fighting fur-ball which seemed to be cemented to its back. The snake heaved upwards. It lurched down, crashing down and the commotion brought the Little Old Witch to her senses.

By the time she could see straight the battle was over. The snake was dead and Velvet Paws sat beside it with

quivering whiskers and twitching ears and flexing claws.
"Did you save my life from that snake?" asked the Little
Old Witch.

"I did," mewed Velvet Paws. "I fell off your broomstick
into the tree," she said. "When the snake attacked you I
dropped on its back. That's all!"

"You must be rewarded, brave Velvet Paws," crooned
the Little Old Witch. "I'll make some magic so that you
and every kitten afterwards will be able to jump from a
height and land safely on four paws. How would you like
that gift?"

Velvet Paws was not impressed by the promise. The
Little Old Witch's magic never worked properly. Yet, for
once, it did. And it's still working to this day. Cats can turn
while falling to make a safe landing, just as long as there is
room for the cat to twist over.

WISH I
COULD
LAND ON
MY FOUR
PAWS !

A SPELL FOR GOOD LUCK
A Good Luck Charm

This spell may or may not work even if all its ingredients can be found. Then there is the extra trouble of finding a well. And at what time of the day should the words be spoken? Should they be whispered, shouted, or chanted? Who knows!

Three white stones
And three black pins
Three yellow gowans
Off the green.
Into the well
With a One, Two, Three!
And a fortune, a fortune,
Come to me!

WITCH'S BREW

Any number of
players may join
in this game, but
first find a cauldron
to hold your brew of bubbling
frothing poisonous broth. A big
supermarket carton will do. One player
becomes the leader. The others join hands to
circle the cauldron while the leader tries to
pull a player out of the circle to the cauldron.
If a player knocks the pot, every one
must quickly shout, *"Poison!"* That
person becomes the next leader.
And so the game goes on
for as long as it's fun.
Play it on grass and look
after smaller people who
join in the game.

PUPPET WITCH

Make a witch from a leg of a stocking, or a pair of panty-hose. Black or green will look good.

Fill the toe with scraps of fabric, foam filling, cotton wool, or chopped up panty-hose. Tie it off and you have the witch's head.

Paste or sew on eyes cut from felt, fabric or paper. Give her a mouth, nose and eyebrows. These can be stitched with coloured threads.

The witch needs hair. Sew on string or shreds of an unravelled stocking or panty-hose.

Cut off the surplus leg below the witch's head. You need to leave enough to cover your hand, so watch that.

Push a paddle-pop stick into the head's filling and use it to work your puppet.

The witch can wear a hat. Cut a circle of paper and roll it into a cone shape. Trim it to size and decorate.

PEANUT PUPPETS

Often when shelling peanuts you'll find that some of the shells slip over your finger tips. Keep these. Paint or draw faces on the shells and in two minutes you'll have a family of peanut puppets.

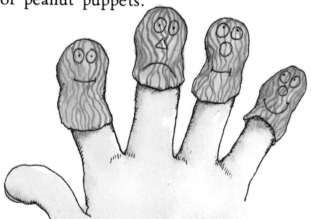

SOCK PUPPET

Sometimes socks are lost and never seen again. Make use of the odd socks as puppets. Just push one hand down as far as the toe. If the sock is small enough let your thumb fill the heel. If not, use your thumb to pucker the sock until it makes a mouth when you close your hand over the thumb. That's all there is to a sock puppet, unless you want to sew on button eyes and a fringe of braid, or other decorations.

KILKENNY CATS

There were two cats of Kilkenny,
Each thought there was one cat too many,
So they fought and they fit,
And they scratched and they bit,
Till, excepting their nails
And the tips of their tails
Instead of two cats, there weren't any.

TWO RED, ROUND CAKES

Somewhere, in the hills of Japan, lived a very large ginger cat and a very small tabby cat, and happy they were together until the day they found two rice cakes. The very large ginger cat had a small rice cake. The very small tabby had a large rice cake, so big that she could hardly hold it in two paws.

"I should have the bigger cake," said Ginger. "I'm bigger than you so I need more to eat."

"Not at all!" purred Tabby. "I need more to eat so that I shall grow."

"*Meeerowww!*" howled Ginger. "Greedy-gutz!"

"Guzzle-pot! Gorger! Fat Belly!" screamed Tabby.

"Oh! Fat-face! String Tail! Skinny Cat!" Ginger shouted back, then showing all of his teeth, he snarled. "Give me that big cake."

Tabby clutched the cake close and hissed, "I won't!" Then she turned in a flash and nipped behind a tree.

Ginger went after her. Round the tree and round the tree they chased. And who was chasing who? It was hard to tell. It ended in a howling, spitting, scratching cat-fight which went on until they were both out of breath. "Ffffighting won't solve our problem," puffed Ginger. "We must go to the Wise Monkey in the forest. He will decide that I should have the bigger cake."

"I found it. He will let me keep it," said Tabby. "Bring
your cake and we'll ask his advice."

With the cakes in their mouths they hurried through
trees, jumped logs, slipped through grass and scurried under
vines to the Wise Monkey in his tree. "Hand me the cakes,"
said Monk. "I'll settle your quarrel."

"You must both have an equal share," he nodded as he
took the cakes. "U-ahhh! This one is definitely bigger."
Monk held up Tabby's cake and took a bite from its side.
"Both cakes should be the same size now," he told the cats.
He held them together. Ginger's cake was the bigger now!
"I'll soon fix that," he said and he took a bit from Ginger's
cake. "Both cakes should *now* be the same size," he told
them.

They were not. Tabby's cake was bigger again. So
Monkey kept taking bites from each cake in turn. Bite, bite,
munch, munch, until ... both cakes were eaten. Not a
crumb was left! "There you are!" chattered Monk, "I told
you that I'd solve the problem. Both cakes are gone, so
that's it!" And Monk climbed to a higher branch to swing
away from the cats' sight.

"Ourrrrr!" howled the greedy pair. "He's eaten our
cakes!" Now we've nothing to eat! *"Ourrrrr!"*

And Ginger and Tabby, two hungry and empty-pawed
cats, slunk home. It has been said that they never quarrelled
again, and maybe they didn't.

JUBA

Juba is a singing game to play alone, or
with another child, or lots of friends.

Ju - ba this and Ju - ba that,   Ju - ba found a   yel - low cat!

Ju - ba up and Ju - ba down,   Ju - ba run-ning   all a - round!

Another way to play Juba is to match actions to the song's
words. Here are two more verses. You add others and then
the song becomes especially yours.

Juba this and Juba that,   *Clap hands together.*
Juba fed his yellow cat,   *Slap hands against thighs.*
Juba up and Juba down,   *Clap against your partner's hands,*
Juba running all around!   *or clap your own together.*
Juba this and Juba that,   *Run about your partner, or run in*
Juba stroked his yellow cat.   *a little circle.*
Juba up and Juba down,
Juba running all around!

Repeat the song and its movements as many times as you
like. Each time sing and move faster. You'll end up falling
over, so Juba is best played outside, on grass.

CATS' EYES

Look deep into Pussy's eyes,
Look well when she mews.
Whatever she is saying,
No doubt is very true.

"Cats can see in the dark," some people will declare. Cats do have 'night' eyes but whether these eyes are blue, or green, or topaz yellow, cats cannot see in total darkness. But in a dim light cats see better than most animals.

Their sharp vision makes cats excellent judges of distances and a cat will seldom overshoot its goal.

> Pussy jump high,
> Pussy jump low,
> Pussy jump safely,
> Wherever you go.

A cat stares unblinkingly with a steady fixed gaze. It's a good time to observe its eyes, without needing to touch the cat.

Do the pupils of cat's eyes become smaller in bright light? Do they grow larger in a dim light?

That's something to find out.

THE BOY WHO DREW CATS

There is a time, in Japan, when cherry trees dress the countryside with boughs of pale pink blossoms and Spring is welcomed. It was at such a time that a farmer took his son to a temple where he might learn to become a priest.

From that day the boy rose early each morning to begin the tasks which the priests had set for him. He rang the bell to awaken the yellow-robed ones from their slumbers. He rolled up their sleeping mats. He cleaned their sandals and he filled their bowls with rice. He did all of that and he did it well. He also studied his lessons, and then, he spent his spare time drawing cats. He drew nothing but cats! Cats sleeping, cats stretching, cats eating, cats hunting, cats yawning, cats stalking, cats lapping, cats walking, cats running! Cats! Cats! Cats! And kittens, too! He drew on parchment and on rice paper with a piece of charcoal. He drew in the dust on the ground and once, he scratched on a large fleshy lotus leaf with a thorn.

The Priests of the Yellow Robes noted his drawings. They saw that they were excellent. They decided that he would make a better artist than a priest and they asked him to leave the temple.

The boy, who was named Yoda, did not want to shame his father because he had failed to become a priest. So, he did not return to his home, but wandered down the mountainside, going from village to village.

One nightfall found him near a large temple. Perhaps the priests there were in need of a boy to help with their tasks?

A light gleamed under the temple door but no one answered the boy's knock. Yoda pushed the door and it opened slowly. He saw a dust-covered floor, a sleeping mat by a screen, some low tables and a large cabinet. That was all! The temple was empty of priests.

"I'll wait until they return," thought Yoda and while he waited he swept the dust and leaves from the temple, moving aside the screen to do so.

It was a bare screen. The boy sat on the mat and looked at the screen for a long time, thinking how he could decorate it. Then, hardly realizing what he was doing, he took a piece of charcoal from his robe and began to draw cats. Cats, cats and cats! Purring cats and fighting cats, washing cats and hunting cats, stretching cats and sleeping cats, feeding cats and mewing cats! Mother cats and kittens

and ferocious old tom cats! He drew until no space was left on the back or the front of the screen.

Yoda was pleased. He stretched out on the mat, feeling drowsy, yet not falling asleep. For some reason he did not feel at ease. Why had the priests not returned to their temple? The hour was now late. He listened for approaching footsteps but heard none. It was silent inside the temple and it was silent outside the temple. Strangely silent! Yoda began to feel afraid.

He left the sleeping mat and went to the cupboard. It was large enough to hold him. Yoda climbed into it, settled on a shelf and drew the door closed. He was able to sleep.

The boy slept soundly, hearing nothing during the night. "I will go and ring the temple bell," he thought when he woke.

Yoda pushed open the cupboard door and jumped to the floor. He stood still, throwing up his arms in astonishment. At his feet, amongst pieces of broken lamp and furniture, lay a rat, a huge and monstrous rat — dead in a pool of blood!

Yoda took a step backwards, staring at the animal. "Such an animal would not have died without a great fight!" he said. "Yet I heard nothing in the night!" He looked about in wonder, half-expecting to see a warrior, exhausted and wounded.

He saw only the screen still standing where he had left it. But the drawings of the cats — they were *not* as he had drawn them!

Yoda ran to the screen. Each sharp black line or furry smudge was as he had drawn, but now each cat's mouth was stained blood red. "The cats ... the cats killed the great rat!" Yoda said softly.

He ran from the temple. He rang the bell. Its peals brought villagers rushing up the mountainside to the temple. "Who rang the bell?" they were shouting.

"I did!" Yoda called back. "I needed shelter for the night."

"You slept there? In the temple?" The villagers were amazed. "And you are still alive? The Monster Rat did not kill you!"

"It is dead," Yoda told them and showed them the rat.

"That monster drove away the priests," they told Yoda. "You have killed it and the priests may return."

"I didn't kill the rat," Yoda explained and he showed them the cats on the screen.

"You are an artist of greatness," they told Yoda and bowed to him. "Your cats are like real cats. And your skill must have given them magical powers to save the temple. Therefore, your screen must never be removed from where it stands." The villagers bowed again, asking to hear the story of the cats once more.

And later, Yoda did become a very great artist, most famous for his drawings of cats.

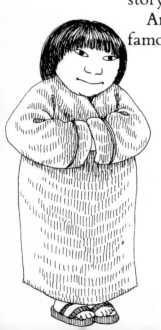

DRAW OR PAINT

Yoda used charcoal to draw. So can you. Pieces of burnt-black stick, charred wood or barbecue coals will draw black lines. Smudge them with a finger for delicate shadings. You'll end up with dirty hands, of course.

Draw on dampened paper with chalk for a velvety look. Bind two or three sticks of chalk together and experiment with different colours.

Shave broken crayons into thin slivers. Wind some sticky-tape about a finger, sticky side out, and pick up the shavings on the tape. Try drawing that way. The ends of coloured candles can be used, too.

Rub layers of crayons over paper then scratch a drawing with a paper clip, a metal knitting needle, or a sharply pointed stick. Try using differently coloured layers of crayon.

Paint on dampened paper. Try using small amounts of food colouring for pale shades.

Draw with a candle. Paint over the drawing with a dark colour. What will happen?

Draw with a tube of glue. Drip it from the nozzle then sprinkle sand over the drawing.

Draw with a sponge, or a dish-mop, or toothbrush, cotton balls, straws, corks. Use the end of a matchbox, a plastic fork, a straw or bottle top.

Experiment! Experiment!

Draw in lemon juice with a cotton bud, or twirl a scrap of a paper tissue about a match. Let it dry, then iron with a warm iron. What has happened?

101

CLEVER TOM

Bang! Crash! Chitter-chatter! *Wallop! Slap*-clatter-*flop!*

The noise was enough to wake sleeping owls and it certainly startled old Tom the cat, who was snoozing on his sunny doorstep. He squinted up at the gang of monkeys in the tree above him. Then they spied him.

Down the tree they slithered. They tweeked his tail, stroked his fur the wrong way, tickled his nose with a feather, poked at him with long fingers, or dangled wrong-side up and just out of reach of his paws.

"*Mow!*" said Tom. Oh, he was a very angry cat! He waved the tip of his tail in annoyance. "All right, you monkeys!" he growled. "Do whatever you like, but let me warn you, do *not* touch that bell over there." Tom nodded towards a wasps' nest under the eaves of the house.

"What bell?" chattered the monkeys, alert and interested.

"*That* bell!" And Tom looked straight up at the wasps' nest. "It belongs to this house. If you ring it there's no knowing what will happen. That bell should only be rung on very special occasions," said Tom, narrowing his eyes to slits. "Take my advice and behave yourselves. Don't ring it."

"Don't ring it! Don't ring it-ring-ring-ring-it!" shrilled the monkeys. "Just watch us!" And up the tree they went, scrambling over each other to swing across to the roof of the house.

"This is when I make myself scarce," thought Tom and he stepped inside the house. Just in time, too!

Whack! Thump! Slap-slap-slap! The monkeys hit the bell-nest with sticks or hands, even feet.

Zzz! Zzzzz! ZzzZZZZ! Furious insects poured from the nest. *Zzzzzzzzzz!* Sting! Sting! And more stings! The wasps punished the monkeys for disturbing their house. *Ouch! Oooh! Slap-scramble!* The monkeys shrieked and yelled as they scurried pell-mell to the river. *Splash! Slosh!* They jumped into the water and escaped from the angry wasps.

And Tom? He tip-toed from the house, settled on the step in the sun with his tail over his nose. And there, he drowsed away the rest of the afternoon, free of monkey business.

TOM IS ALMOST AS CLEVER AS ME!

MONKEY BUSINESS

Cut the pieces for the monkey from stiff cardboard, using our monkey as a pattern.

Link his joints with split pins. Now the monkey's arms and legs can be pushed into different positions.

Give him a face. Give him a tail from a scrap of leather or material. Glue it into place.

Monkey, Monkey, Woo!
More than one or two
Swing in jungle trees,
By tails, hands or knees.
Monkey, Monkey, Woo!
What else can they do?
Pull funny faces,
As if they were *you!*

LONG TIME AGO

Once there was a lit-tle kit-ty, White as the snow, She went out to hunt a mous-ie, Long time a-go.

Two black eyes had little kitty,
Black as a crow,
And they spied a little mousie,
Long time ago.

Four soft paws had little kitty,
Soft as bread dough,
And they caught the little mousie,
Long time ago.

Nine pearl teeth had little kitty,
All in a row,
And she bit the little mousie,
Long time ago.

When the kitty bit the mousie,
Mousie cried, "Ohh!"
But she got away from kitty,
Long time ago.

105

Long ago, there lived a wise king who is remembered to this very day. His name was Solomon and he wore a wonderful ring which gave him the power to understand the language of animals.

The Pharaoh, King of Egypt, heard of Solomon's wisdom and the power of his ring. "I will send to him an honoured gift, a golden cat," said the Pharaoh. That was an honoured gift, indeed. An Egyptian cat was more than a pet, more than a hunter of rats and mice. The Egyptians then believed that their cats were related to the cat-gods. And the cat chosen for Solomon was a handsome, long-legged, lithe animal with golden-red fur which felt thick and springy under stroking fingers. Each fine hair was darkened at its tip as if pencilled, so her coat shimmered when she moved in the sunshine, or fire-light. She looked up at Solomon with eyes as green as summer leaves glistening with morning dew.

He was delighted with his cat. He kept her with him. They talked together and dined together and enjoyed each other's company so much that the Golden Cat learned to hold a candle by the king's plate to light his food.

And guests invited to Solomon's banquets were charmed by the golden cat, even a man named Morolf, although he said, "I have watched the Golden One, O King. She holds the candle steadily in her paws, but I am sure that I can make her forget her task."

"You can?" smiled Solomon. "I would like to see that."

"This evening then, my lord, I shall test your cat," said Morolf.

And that evening Morolf came to the banquet table with three plump mice hidden in the folds of his robe. Soon the king entered and the golden cat took up a lighted candle in her paws. And Morolf watched as she lit the dishes being served to Solomon.

It was not until a servant placed a bowl of figs on the table that Morolf crept a hand over its edge to release the first mouse. It skittered from his fingers, fleeing across the table in front of the cat. She looked but she didn't move and the mouse disappeared over the opposite table-edge.

Morolf released the second mouse. It scurried closer to the golden cat. Within paw reach! She clutched her candle as firmly as ever and stared beyond its light into the shadows of the room.

The third mouse darted from Morolf's hand.

The golden cat's ears pressed downwards. Her eyes glittered. Her whiskers twitched. Her tail flicked so gently it hardly moved the length of a fingernail, and then only its tip. And the golden cat dropped the candle. She pounced on the mouse.

Morolf turned to the king. "O Lord Solomon, you may understand the language of animals through the power of your ring, but you cannot change the nature of your cat. She was born to hunt mice."

Solomon bowed to Morolf, smiled at him, then answered with dignified grace, "Morolf, noble friend, what you have proved is that the wisdom of God is greater than that of a king, such as I. Indeed, He who created the cat with her purpose, also created man, who in his foolishness cannot improve upon God's work."

And those words are as true now as when Solomon spoke them.

THE ROSE IS RED

The rose is red, the grass is green,
Serve Queen Bess, our noble queen,
Kitty, the spinner
Will sit down to dinner
And eat the leg of a frog.
All you good people
Look over the steeple
And see the cat chased by the dog.

THE OWL AND THE PUSSY-CAT

The Owl and the Pussy-cat went to sea
   In a beautiful pea-green boat,
They took some honey, and plenty of money
   Wrapped up in a five-pound note.
The Owl looked up to the stars above,
   And sang to a small guitar,
"O lovely Pussy, O Pussy, my love,
   What a beautiful Pussy you are,
       You are,
       You are!
What a beautiful Pussy you are!"

110

Pussy said to the Owl, "You elegant fowl,
  How charmingly sweet you sing!
Oh! let us be married, too long we have tarried:
  But what shall we do for a ring?"
They sailed away, for a year and a day,
  To the land where the Bong-tree grows;
And there in a wood a Piggy-wig stood,
  With a ring at the end of his nose,
      His nose,
      His nose,
  With a ring at the end of his nose.

"Dear Pig, are you willing to sell for one shilling
  Your ring?" Said the Piggy, "I will."
So they took it away, and were married next day
  By the turkey who lives on the hill.
They dined on mince and slices of quince,
  Which they ate with a runcible spoon;
And hand·in hand, on the edge of the sand,
  They danced by the light of the moon,
      The moon,
      The moon,
  They danced by the light of the moon.

Edward Lear.

BEANS IN A BAG

Firmly woven scraps of materials can be made into bean bags. Velvet, felt, linen, fur fabric, braids, fringings, buttons and other oddments can be used for trimmings. Plaits of wool or cotton can become animals' tails or hair. Shorter lengths are useful as embroidery threads.

A round bean bag is quickly made, but try a basic wedge shape to make an Owl and a Pussy-cat, the Piggy-wig or any other animal.

For each animal cut two pieces of material which are the same size. Its bottom and sides measure about 150 mm but the sides slope into the top which is shorter, about 90 mm.

On one piece of cloth sew, glue, embroider or paint on the animal's features.

Match both pieces together and firmly stitch about the edges. Leave an opening at the top to fill the animal with dried beans, or dried peas, rice or lentils. Stitch the opening firmly so that the filling can't dribble out.

The edges of the seams can be fringed if you like.

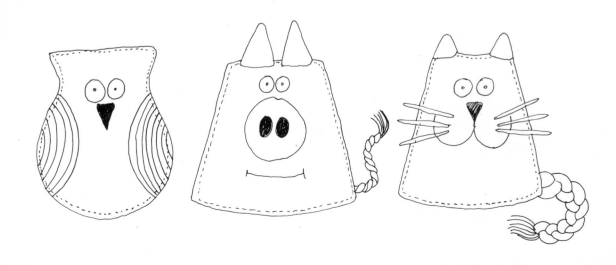

THE CAT CAME BACK

Now old Mis - ter John - son had troub-les of his own, He

had an old yel - low cat that would - n't leave its home. He tried

ev - 'ry thing he knew to keep the cat a - way, He

took it up to Can - a - da and told it for to stay...

Refrain

But the cat came back the ver - y next day, The old

cat came back, Thought he was a gon - ner, The

cat came back 'cause he could - n't stay a - way.

113

He gave the boy a dollar for to set the cat afloat,
He took him up the river in a sack in a boat.
Well the fishing it was fine 'til the news got around,
That the boat was missing and the boy was drowned.
Repeat Refrain

On the telegraph wire the birds were sitting in a bunch,
He saw six or seven, said he'd have 'em for his lunch.
He climbed softly to the top and put his foot on the wire,
Well his fur was scorched off and his tail caught fire.
Repeat Refrain

Well they threw him in the kennel when the dog was
  asleep,
And the bones of cats lay piled in a heap.
Well the kennel bust apart and the dog flew out the side,
With his ears chewed off and holes in his side.
Repeat Refrain

This is a nonsense song from America. Goodness knows
who first wrote it! It is true, however, that some cats will
travel long distances on foot to find a way home. Often a
journey takes weeks. How does a cat find its way? See if
you can discover this for yourself. Does it follow sound?
Does it follow smell? Here's a clue. A cat relies upon its
hearing to help it find its way about.

THE MAGIC RING

In the long-ago days when anything could happen Hans owned a gold ring, and it was a magic ring. It gave him everything that he needed; not too much and not too little. Just enough! And Hans kept the power of the ring as his secret, never telling anyone about it, not even Gretel, his plump little wife. *U-ah!* That was a mistake! A big mistake! Gretel sold the ring. And dear, oh dear, she didn't get much for it either! Just a couple of copper coins! And as you know, it *was* gold.

The coins soon were spent and Hans and Gretel grew poorer and poorer as each day passed. There was no longer milk to be spared for the cat. No bones for the dog! Hardly any bread and broth for Hans. That's how bad things were.

Kitlin Puss and Riff-raff had never been so wretched in their lives. "This is no life for a cat," mewed Kitlin. "And no life for a dog," barked Riff-raff. "All our troubles began when Gretel sold the ring," said Kitlin. "Then we'll have to get it back," decided Riff-raff. "Howwwwww?" mewed Kitlin. "Howwwww?"

Riff-raff didn't know.

I HAVE MANY CAT FRIENDS

"I'll think about it," said Kitlin and she thought for two minutes. "Riff-raff, I was there when Gretel sold the ring. She was cheated. She was not given enough money in exchange."

"I know, I know, I know!" said Riff-raff. "How in the world can we get the ring back?"

"The cheat put the ring inside a box. He keeps it on a table inside his house," mewed Kitlin. "But as clever as I am, Riff-raff, I don't know how I can get the ring from its box."

"If you caught a mouse, Kitlin, it could chew a hole in the box," said Riff-raff.

"Mmmmmm, a sensible plan," decided Kitlin, and she ran off to catch a mouse.

Before long she was back with the mouse dangling below her whiskers and she set off with Riff-raff to the house of the man with the ring.

They came to a river. "Mmm, mmmmm, ma mant met mover," mewed Kitlin with her mouthful of mouse.

Riff-raff nodded, knowing that she couldn't cross the river. Kitlin absolutely hated to wet her feet so he invited her to climb onto his back. She did. Riff-raff then swam the river and Kitlin kept her paws dry.

She hurried on to the house of the man with the ring, and jumped in through a window. "Mousiekin, gnaw a hole in that box on the table," she said. "Bring me the ring from inside it. After that you may go free. I won't eat you up."

The mouse nibbled. She *nibbled!* She nibbled for dear life. She nibbled until a hole, the size of your middle finger was chewed into the box. Kitlin-puss pushed in a paw and hauled out the ring. *Zerp!* The mouse skit-scaddled! She was off to goodness knows where, before Kitlin could change her mind.

116

Kitlin, however, was busy picking up the ring in her mouth and that was not easy for a cat with paws. "Fingers do have their uses," she mewed.

She managed it at last, jumped from the window with the ring in her mouth and ran to the river, with Riff-raff loping along beside her. She climbed on his back. He swam across and Kitlin didn't get her feet wet. And while Riff-raff shook and rolled himself dry, Kitlin sped on to home.

She used the very best of short-cuts. Up over walls! Under hedges! Over roof-tops! Along fences until she was home with the ring.

Kitlin dropped it at Hans' feet. Oh, that cunning little cat! She was rewarded at once. Hans stroked and petted her and called her 'clever one'. "Kitlin has brought back my lost ring," he called to Gretel.

"I wonder how she did that?" said Gretel. "She must have cream at once."

And cream Kitlin had. It was being poured into her saucer when Riff-raff limped into the kitchen. A bedraggled and footsore Riff-raff. "Where have you been, you good-for-nothing?" scolded Hans. "Where were you when it was time to bring in the cow?" He hunted Riff-raff from the house. "No dinner for you, fleabag!"

Well, you know where Riff-raff had been. Kitlin knew too. Stretched out on Hans' knee, she gazed into the fire as if she'd agreed with her master's treatment of his dog. The sly puss!

Riff-raff was angry with her. He spent the night, cold and hungry in the field and he grew extremely angry. So angry that when Kitlin minced out of the kitchen door the next morning he made for her. *"Woooof!"* He chased her across the garden. Up a tree she went. And she was safe enough there. Just as well! Riff-raff threatened to grab her by the neck and shake and shake her until her ears fell off. Whether he ever did catch her, I've not heard, but many dogs have chased cats ever since. I expect you have noticed that?

CAT AND DOG GAME

Any number of children can play, even adults can join in if you invite them. First, select one player to be the *Cat*. Now decide who will be the *Dog*. The others make a circle about *Cat*. *Dog* prowls around the outside.

Everyone ready? Right! *Dog* tries to break through the circle of tightly held hands. He wants that cat! And he barks and howls so that everyone knows.

Cat mews and hopes that he won't break through the circle.

When *Dog* does manage to reach *Cat*, the cat must join the players in the circle. *Dog* now becomes the cat. He also decides who will be the next *Dog*, picking someone from the circle. Right? And so the game goes on and on, until you are tired of playing it.

THERE WAS A CROOKED MAN

There was a crooked man
Who walked a crooked mile,
And found a crooked sixpence
Upon a crooked stile.
He bought a crooked cat
That caught a crooked mouse,
And they all lived together
In a little crooked house.

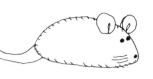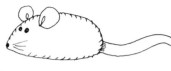

FUN-MOUSE

This little creature isn't a little crooked mouse but a fun-mouse. Fill it with cat-nip for a favourite cat to play with, day after day. It can be filled with cotton-wool or synthetic filling, then it's a pin cushion or a small child's toy.

You will need some scraps of felt, velvet or a sturdy vinyl, woollen or cotton material. You will need sewing thread, a black marking pen, and the filling.

Cut an oval shape from the felt. That's a stretched out circle shape. Your oval should measure about 10cm in length and 7cm across the middle which is the fattest part of the oval. This is the body.

Cut another oval. It is smaller because it is the under part of the mouse's body. It should measure about 10cm in length and 5cm across the middle.

Cut *two* tiny circles for the ears. 3cm across is a good size.

Cut a tail. Make it long and skinny, about 17cm. Keep it at least 1cm at one end. Taper away to nothing for the tail-tip.

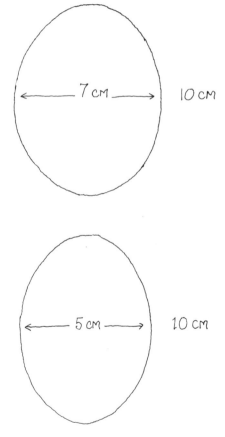

7 CM   10 CM

5 CM   10 CM

EARS

TAIL

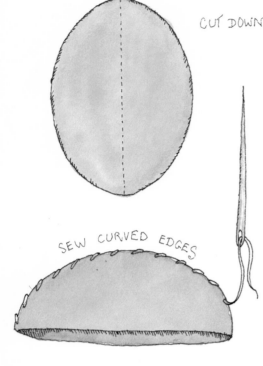

CUT DOWN CENTRE LINE

SEW CURVED EDGES

SEW SECOND OVAL TO BODY

LEAVE OPENING FOR TAIL AND FILLING

CUT PIE-SHAPED PIECE FROM EACH EAR

Now you're ready to stitch, but first cut the larger oval into two *even* pieces by folding it down the centre to make a guide-line. Sew the *curved* edges together. Use an over-sewing stitch if you can.

Stitch the body to the second oval. Leave an opening for the tail and the filling. Stuff your mouse until it's fat and well-fed looking. Now, push in the tail at the wider end. Stitch it into position and stitch up the opening to keep the filling in place.

From each ear cut away a tiny pie-shaped piece. Overlap these cut edges into a pleat and sew the ear to Mouse's head by anchoring it down by the pleat. You'll have a rounded mousie ear. Sew on the second ear.

Give the mouse eyes and a nose by using a marker pen. Embroider or draw on whiskers if you think your mouse needs these.

TAILOR MOUSE

Gib, the hunter caught a fat little mouse. And a very smart mouse it was. "Gib, before you eat me, I think I should make you a suit of clothes," it squeaked. "I'm a first-class sewer. It is a pity to waste my skill."

"Humph!" grunted Gib. He looked at his fur. He had known it to look better. Yes, it was shabby. Not very much, but moth-eaten a little here and there! And there were a couple of tears and patchy places. Yes, he would look more handsome in a new coat. "Make me a leather coat, Kid," said Gib. "I'll get you some leather."

The mouse scampered home and the next day Gib was shouting down her hole. "Hey, you! Mouse! Here's the leather! Make a coat from it, will you? After that, I'll eat you."

"There's not enough leather here to make a coat," Mouse said, peeking from her hole. "However, by cutting it carefully I shall be able to make you a pair of trousers."

A cat in trousers? In pants? Gib had heard of cats' pyjamas but not trousers. He would be the only cat in the town with trousers. He liked the idea of that. "Make trousers then, Kid," he growled and swaggered away.

Back at the mouse-hole next morning he wanted to know, "Where's that pair of strides, Kid?"

"Sorry, Gib! There wasn't enough leather for trousers. I'll make you a vest," promised Mouse from deep inside her hole.

Maw! Other cats had vests! White furry vests were very popular. Gib had seen many a cat sticking his chest out to show off his vest. Vests were common. Still, a leather vest *was* different. Very smart! He, Gib, would start a new fashion. "Okay, Kid!" he bawled out and stalked off, looking down his nose at his chest and imagining what a handsome cat he would be next day.

When he called the next morning Mouse sounded tearful. "I . . . I couldn't m-manage a v-vest, Gib. W-will I make a l-little l-leather c-cap?"

A cat in a hat! Gib had never seen a sight like that. It sounded hunky dory! Yes, he'd settle for that. "Make a cap, Kid!" he boomed to Mouse and took a few fancy dance steps away from the hole, then wondered if Mouse would make holes for his ears, or would he flatten them under the cap.

124

Gib told everyone that was catty about his cap but he was a wild-wild cat when he next heard from Mouse. "Gib! There ... there wasn't-enough-leather-for-a-cap!" she called from her hole. Gib was sure she sniffed, then hiccupped before saying softly, "I'm sorry, Gib."

"And so you should be," howled Gib. "I'll pull your whiskers one by one. You've chopped and changed enough to make my blood boil. I could have eaten you days ago. What are the other cats going to say? They expect to see me wearing a cap!"

"I could make you some gloves," whispered Mouse.

Gloves! Gib had heard of kittens in mittens and some cats flashed about in white socks. The show-offs! Gib had never seen a cat wearing leather gloves. Mmmm! Gloves would do. "Get on with it then. Make those gloves. I'm skinny with hunger and this time I intend to eat you whether the gloves are finished or not!" Gib growled every word down the mouse-hole and Mouse heard each one. Then he marched off, waving his tail. He *was* going to eat that mouse, gloves or no gloves.

Next morning when he arrived at the mouse-hole what did he see but a note with a pebble on top of it so that it wouldn't blow away. It must have been an important note to be left so carefully. And it was a lucky thing that Gib could read. "Gib!" it said, "I have gone to China to make trousers and coats, vests and caps and gloves for the Chinese cats." And it was signed? *Mouse.* She was a very smart mouse, wouldn't you agree?

SIX LITTLE MICE

Six little mice sat down to spin,
Pussy passed by, and she peeped in.
"What are you at, my little men?"
"Making coats for gentlemen."
"Shall I come in and bite off your threads?"
"No, no, Miss Pussy, you'll snip off our heads."
"Oh, no, I'll not, I'll help you to spin."
"That may be so, but you can't come in!"

MOUSE-HOUND

Hundreds of mice, thousands of mice had moved into the village of Schilda. Brazenly impudent mice! They even ran about in broad daylight, helping themselves to whatever they fancied. They were so bold they chewed up everything and anything they could get their teeth into; and they nested in shoes and cupboards and the mayor's hat. The invasion of mice grew worse and as each day passed, the Good Men of Schilda grew frantic with worry. What could they do?

Get a cat? Yes, yes! Except . . . except that the Good Men of Schilda had never heard of a cat!

Then, right out of the blue of a sunny morning, into the village of Schilda strode a bad-baggage of a pedlar, with a tabby cat under an arm. "What kind of an animal is that?" asked the inn-keeper. "I've never seen its like before."

"This is a mouse-hound!" answered the pedlar, hiding his joke behind a smile.

"A mouse-hound, eh!" said the inn-keeper. "What can it do?"

Well, he had hardly spoken the words than a mouse skittered across the floor. The mouse-hound leapt from the pedlar's arm as if she were flying, pounced on the mouse and that was the end of that mouse.

The inn-keeper gawked, his eyes round with disbelief. Then he shook his head. Next thing, he was racing to the Council Chambers yelling the glad news of the mouse-hound's way with a mouse. The Mayor and the Councillors, tripping over their robes, scrambled out of the Council Chambers into the inn, demanding to buy the mouse-hound.

"I really don't want to sell my animal," complained the pedlar. "I'm very fond of her. Besides, she is a rare beast with many accomplishments."

"The town is infested with mice. We will give you fifty gold pieces for the mouse-hound," offered the Mayor.

"I don't know," sighed the pedlar. "Perhaps ... perhaps I could think of parting with her as you need her skills so desperately, but on the other hand..."

The pedlar was ready to bargain but the Mayor said anxiously, "We'll pay you another fifty gold pieces, just as soon as we can save it. Please sell your mouse-hound," he pleaded.

If the Good Men of Schilda had but fifty gold pieces, then to haggle was useless. The pedlar pulled a face which was sad with regret. "Very well!" he said, "the mouse-hound is yours." And he made a tearful farewell of Tabby.

Five minutes later, he was capering out of the town, kicking up his heels and pitching his cap into the air with whoops of joy, even though his pockets were weighed down with gold.

As for the Good Men of Schilda, they carried their expensive Tabby to the castle where the fattest and sleekest and the largest number of mice frisked, and where the town's grain was stored. "What else does the mouse-hound eat beside mice?" wondered the Mayor. "Someone run after the pedlar. Fetch him back so he may tell us. We must look after our investment in the proper manner."

The fastest runner sped from the village after the pedlar.

The pedlar, the bad-baggage, glanced over his shoulder

and saw that he was being followed. "Zooks!" he whispered. "The Good Men of Schilda have discovered that I've sold them an old farm cat. They want their money back." And the rogue took to his heels, sprinting off like an athlete. "Stop! Stop!" shouted his pursuer. "Stop! What . . . does . . . the . . . mouse-hound . . . eat?"

If the pedlar heard he certainly didn't spare his breath to answer. He ran faster, pulling further and further ahead of the puffing villager who slowed to a limp because of a stitch in his side. "Oh-oh-oh!" he panted and turned back to the village of Schilda. "Oh-oh! If the mouse-hound eats mice with such relish, then . . . then, oh dear! it will also eat our cattle," he thought. And you can well imagine how that thought terrified him, but his next thought was worse! "And when it's eaten the cattle, it will eat *us*!" he gasped. It was enough to set him running again and he was very foot-sore and weary when he hobbled into the castle. "Good Men of Schilda!" he quavered. "I must tell you! The mouse-hound will be the end of us!" He was in a dreadful state. Trembling! Shaking! And so were the Good Men of Schilda when they heard his news.

"We have spent good gold on the mouse-hound," declared the Mayor when he had calmed a little. "We must find a way of dealing with it before it has a chance to eat us."

"Burn down the castle!" shouted the Councillors. "It will be better to suffer its loss and the grain, than to lose our lives."

And burn the castle they did.

Tabby, using her claws as hooks, jumped to a safe landing from a castle window, to the windowsill of the next-door house. She escaped the flames and sat grooming her fur.

The Good Men of Schilda watched her, growing more afraid of their mouse-hound as each minute passed.

They tried to catch her, then lure her from her sill. She ignored them. "Burn down the house!" ordered the Mayor.

Whhhrrt! Swoooosh! It went up in flames and clouds of smoke.

Tabby jumped to the roof of the neighbouring house and calmly washed her face. "She's making ready for an attack!" warned one of the Good Men. He thrust his spear at her. It missed, slid downwards and propped against the wall of the house. Their mouse-hound stepped daintily onto the shaft and with one foot after the other ran down it, neatly to the ground.

The Good Men of Schilda back-back-backed away from the spear, then falling over each other, shouting with panic they bolted for hiding places, with shaking legs and fast-beating hearts.

130

The fire spread to the next house, then the next until the village was ablaze.

The Good Men of Schilda now bravely led their wives and children and all their relatives into the forest to a refuge amongst the trees. They set up a guard against the terrible and ferocious mouse-hound, in case she followed them there.

Tabby did not. She had the remains of the village to herself, except for the mice who had survived the fire. She may be living there yet for all the Good Men of Schilda know. They never returned to their old village but speedily built a new one. And for years afterwards they congratulated themselves by re-telling the events which had saved them from the monstrous, man-eating mouse-hound. And now you know the story, too.

OLD MOTHER MITCHELL

Old Moth - er Mit - chell she has lost her cat. She

cries at the win - dow "Who will bring it back?" It's

sly old Lus - tu - cru who ans - wers to her call, "Go

on, old Moth - er Mit - chell your cat's not lost at all!"

With a song of tra - la - la - la, with a song of tra - la - la -

la, with a song of tra - la - la - la, tra - la - la

DICK WHITTINGTON

When a king called Richard sat upon the English throne, Dick Whittington was told that the streets of London were paved with gold. There was no one to tell Dick that the streets were cobblestones, or tracks of mud, so he begged a wagon-ride and to London he went.

Dick ran through the streets, thinking at any moment he would reach those which were gold. He ran until it was dark and all he found was a sheltered corner where he slept.

The next morning someone gave him a penny to buy food and it kept him from starving for that day. He needed work because there was no gold on the London streets.

Dick worked in a hay field but once the hay was brought in he was as badly off as before. Indeed, he may have starved if he hadn't huddled on the doorstep of the merchant, Mr Fitzwarren.

"Take yourself off before I douse you with dishwater!" shouted the old dame of a cook who saw him there. "Away you go, you lazy rogue!"

She may have drenched him, had not Mr Fitzwarren come home then for his dinner. "Why do you lie there? Are you too lazy to work?" asked Mr Fitzwarren.

"No one will give me work," said Dick. "I am . . . I . . . " He tried to stand up but was too weak from hunger.

Mr Fitzwarren had the dirty little boy taken into his house where he was given both a good wash and a good dinner, then kept there to help the cranky cook until he was well and strong again.

"Look sharp!" she ordered him. "Turn that spit! Clean the dripping pan! Make up the fires! Wash the pots! Scrape the pans! Clean the scullery! Or it will be the worse for you," she threatened and shook her ladle at Dick, or whacked him over the shoulders with it. She laid into him with the broom, too, and anything else she could put her hands upon. And luckily for Dick, the daughter-of-the-house, little Miss Alice, discovered her at it, and ordered her to stop beating Dick.

The cook was only one of Dick's troubles, however. His room was in the garret, at the top of the house, and he was so tormented by rats and mice, he hardly dared to sleep.

Dick bought a cat for one penny and hid her in his garret. And even though he took her part of his dinner each day, she soon rid his room of the rats and mice.

Not long afterwards Dick's master had a ship ready to sail, and it was his custom to allow his servants to send something for trade by his ship. He called his servants into the parlour but Dick did not come with the others. "I will lay down some money for Dick," Miss Alice told her father.

134

"That will not do," Mr Fitzwarren said. "Dick must give something of his own. Bring him to me."

"I don't have anything but a cat," Dick was to explain. "She is all I own."

"Send your cat, then," said Mr Fitzwarren. "She will bring good luck to the ship if she sails with them."

Dick fetched his cat and sorry he was to hand her over.

"What do you think your cat will see in foreign lands?" hissed the cook. "Will she fetch the price of a stick to beat you with?"

Dick sorely missed his cat. Miss Alice gave him money to buy another and the cook teased him as cruelly as before, until Dick could stand it no longer. He decided to run away.

Before anyone stirred in the house, early in the morning of All Hallow's Day, Dick gathered his few belongings into a bundle and walked from the house, as far as Holloway. "Which way to go from London?" he wondered and sat down by the roadside. The very place is still there in London if you look for it. It was then that the six bells of Bow Church began to peel and they seemed to be ringing for him ...

"Turn again, Whittington,
   Thrice Lord Mayor of London!"
"Lord Mayor!" he repeated softly. *"Lord Mayor of London!"* he shouted. "I can put up with that bad tempered cook to be Lord Mayor one day." And Dick was back in the house, busily at work before the cook tramped downstairs to fill the porridge pot.

By then his cat had reached the West Coast of Africa, her ship driven by a storm to Barbary where the dark-skinned Moors lived. The Moors crowded the harbour to see the strange ship and the pale sailors, and indeed, they were anxious to buy the ship's cargo.

The captain, however, insisted upon sending patterns of the best goods to their King and he was invited to dine at the palace. He was given the place of honour upon a gold and silver carpet, then a number of dishes were set before the King and his Queen.

Before one spoonful was served a horde of rats and mice rushed in and gobbled up the food. "I would give half of my kingdom if I could be rid of these pests," said the King. "They eat my food. They even invade my bed chamber."

"There is an animal on board my ship that will rid you of rats and mice," said the captain.

"If this is so, I shall load your ship with gold," said the King. "Bring the creature to me."

Now the captain knew his business. "It would not be convenient for me to part with her. When she leaves my ship, rats and mice will destroy my cargo," he told the King. "However, I will oblige you, Your Majesty."

"Make haste, then. Back to your ship," urged the Queen, "And I shall order another feast to be prepared for your return."

136

The captain, with Puss under his arm, arrived back at the banqueting hall as the rats appeared again to gobble up the second dinner. Puss jumped from his arms and within minutes rats and mice lay dead at her feet. The rest scuttled back to their holes.

"Bring the brave creature to me," called the Queen.

"Puss, puss, puss!" Hearing her name, the cat ran to the captain who scooped her up to hand her to the Queen, but she drew back, afraid now of the killer of rats and mice. "Pussy! Pretty Puss!" said the captain, stroking the cat's neck. "Putty! Putty!" murmured the Queen, gathering enough courage to stroke her, too. "Putty!" she said as the cat was placed in her lap. "Prrrrrt!" answered Puss, settling herself comfortably, then batting a paw at the Queen's rings.

The King was over-joyed to be rid of the rats and mice. He paid the captain ten times more for the cat than he did for the ship's cargo.

The ship sailed for England on a fair wind. And as soon as he had landed the captain went straight to Mr Fitzwarren's counting house. "I bring good news of the ship, Unicorn, and Dick Whittington's cat," he said as he showed the lists of gifts from the Moorish King in exchange for Puss.

"I shall not deprive Dick of a single penny," declared Mr Fitzwarren as he read. "It is his own, earnt by his cat. He will have every farthing of this wealth."

Now Dick was scouring pots for the cook. He was grease and grime to the elbows but Mr Fitzwarren would have him at the counting house without delay. "Your cat was sold to the King of Barbary," Mr Fitzwarren told him. "In return for her you have more riches than I possess in the whole world. Dick, I wish you well."

Dick hardly knew what to do. He begged his master to keep what he pleased, since he owed his fortune to the family's kindness. "No, it is yours," insisted Mr Fitzwarren.

Miss Alice would not accept any of the fortune either, so Dick made a handsome gift to the captain, and to the servants in the house, including the cook.

Then Dick washed and had his hair curled. He dressed in fine clothes and wore a fine hat. He was as grand as any young gentleman who came courting Miss Alice, wanting her to be his sweetheart. Not one of these young men suited Alice and it wasn't long before her father saw that it was Dick she loved. And he saw that Dick loved Alice.

They were married, The Lord Mayor, the Court of Aldermen, the Sheriffs and the richest merchants in London attended the wedding. And Dick and his lady were to live in great splendour and happiness. History tells that he did become Lord Mayor of London, not once but three times, as Bow Bells had predicted. Indeed, Dick was a worthy citizen of his town and when young King Henry came home from his wars in France he knighted him. "Never has a prince had such a subject," the King said. "Never has a subject had such a King," answered Sir Richard Whittington, and perhaps he remembered how as a little boy he had believed the streets of London were paved with gold.

RING-A-LING!

A baby born within the sounds of Bow Bells is called a real Londoner, and one such baby was Her Majesty, Queen Elizabeth.

These play bells won't chime like Dick Whittington's but they will sound pleasantly. Make some for yourself.

Flower Pot Chimes

You will need a small terracotta flower pot which shouldn't be needed by someone else. It should have a sweet tone so make sure it's not cracked.

The flower pot bell needs a tongue, a clanger. Find a heavy glass bead, or a small pebble. Tie it to one end of a nylon string, or cord. Thread the other end through the drainage hole in the pot until the clanger has enough room to swing against the inside. Secure the cord by knotting a stick over the hole on the inside. The rest of the cord can be used to hang the bell, or to hold it. Swing the bell until it clangs. Careful! Don't push too hard! *Ding-dong! Dang!*

Chime Bars

A different sound, like small metal bells, is the tinkling from a chime bar. It is made from a row of nails hung from a board about 33 cm long. The nails should be as big as you can find and each one hung at a different level. Tinkle with a large nail. *Ting-a-ling!*

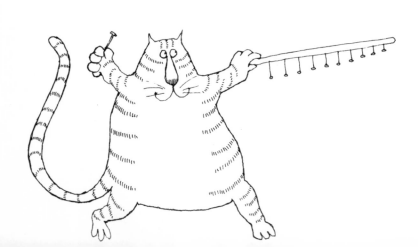

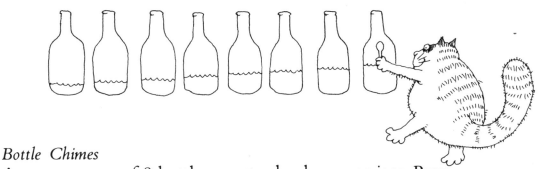

Bottle Chimes

Arrange a row of 8 bottles, or sturdy glasses, or jars. Pour water into each one. Start with a small amount in the first bottle. Add a little more water to each bottle in the row until the last bottle holds the most, yet is not really full. Strike the bottles with a metal spoon. Not too hard! A bottle may break!

Joy Bells

Sew as many small bells as will fit onto strips of felt or tape. Fasten the strips to wrists and ankles with safety pins. You'll make music as you walk, or dance.

Tambourine

You may need help with this one. You can use a paper plate but an old enamel plate or a tin lid will last longer. Holes need to be drilled at equal spacing about the rim. Four holes. Loop cords through the holes. On the ends of the cords fasten metal bottle tops, or joy bells, wooden beads or small cubes of wood. Shake and bang the tambourine.

DING-DONG!

Ding-dong! Ding-dong!
   All the bells are ringing,
Ding-dong! Ding-dong!
   It's a holiday.

Ding-dong! Ding-dong!
   All the birds are singing,
Ding-dong! Ding-dong!
   Let's go out and play.

THE BELLS OF LONDON

Gay go up and gay go down,
To ring the bells of London town.
Halfpence and farthings,
Say the bells of St Martin's.
Oranges and lemons,
Say the bells of St Clement's.
Pancakes and fritters,
Say the bells of St Peter's.
Two sticks and an apple,
Say the bells of Whitechapel.
Kettles and pans,
Say the bells of St Ann's.
You owe me ten shillings,
Say the bells of St Helen's.
When will you pay me?
Say the bells of Old Bailey.
When I grow rich,
Say the bells of Shoreditch.
Pray when will that be?
Say the bells of Stepney.
I am sure I don't know,
Says the great bell of Bow.

KURREMURRE

Little dwarf Katto, loved little dwarf woman Ulva, and they may have married and may have been happy but for Kurremurre. He fancied Ulva for himself. And Kurremurre was a terror. The strongest and most horrible of all the dwarfs ever to live under the hill! He was the richest, too. And the fiercest! And the worst tempered! As if that wasn't enough, he was also the ugliest! Kurremurre bullied the countryside and when he announced that he was to wed with little Ulva she was beside herself with grief.

She clung to Katto and howled, but it did no good. None whatsoever! Kurremurre grabbed Ulva by her long black hair, pushed an iron ring on her finger and roared to the dwarfs to witness the marriage ceremony.

"You're mine now," he snarled, "and don't you forget it, Ulva."

After that there was nothing little dwarf Katto could do but to look upon Ulva for one last time. It was a long,

loving look he gave her. Then he changed himself into a cat and left the hill.

Katto made a handsome cat. A handsome tabby cat! Green eyes shining like emeralds! Black nose like fine leather! Golden fur swirled with black. Fur more beautiful than water-silk! He'd have no trouble finding a comfortable home.

The first house he came to belonged to the farmer, Platt. Katto rubbed a shoulder against the door-post and Platt's wife invited him in. And she gave him a bowl of broth and a cushiony chair by the fire. A grand life began for him, then and there. He had nothing to do but to catch a few mice now and again and purr when he was spoken to by Platt or his Goody. His pleasant pussy-cat life went on for years but all that time Katto never forgot Ulva.

Every Wednesday morning, promptly at eight o'clock, Platt left for market. He was home again for his supper at six in the evening. It was just before six when he came striding into the house on the particular Wednesday that you must hear about.

As usual, Katto jumped from his chair, stretched his long legs then leapt into Platt's lap. As soon as Katto was comfortable, Platt began to eat. One mouthful of pea-soup! Two mouthfuls! Then, what does he do but put down his spoon and laugh so heartily that his stomach shook, disturbing Katto who flicked an ear, then sprang to the floor. Platt laughed so loudly that his Goody stopped eating and looked at him with surprise.

"Have you ever seen a dwarf?" chuckled Platt.

"Never! And I have no wish to see one," she said and put some meat on a saucer for Katto.

"I've never seen one either," said Platt.

"Then that is nothing to laugh about," his Goody told him. "Get on with your dinner."

"Patience, patience, Woman!" Platt told her. "I'll tell you about my journey home. It is worth a laugh. Listen, now. I came as far as that pleasant little hill along the way — we've both seen it a thousand times, or more. And all at once, a pebble hit me on the knee."

"So?" said Mrs Platt. "You must have kicked it up." She began to eat again, and so did Katto who had stopped to stare at Platt when he had mentioned the hill.

"The pebble was *thrown* at me," Platt told her.

She stopped eating. So did Katto. "Who threw the pebble?" his Goody wanted to know.

"I'm coming to that," said Platt. "It was very, very funny!"

"Then get on with your tale. I'm waiting for the funny part."

"The pebble hit me on the knee, as I said. I stopped to rub it," explained Platt.

"You rubbed the *pebble*?" She took another spoonful and Katto daintily picked up a corner of meat.

"No, no, no! I rubbed my knee," said Platt. "Then, as I rubbed I heard a squeak-squeak."

"A mouse, I suppose. A field mouse." The Goody ate and so did Katto.

"It was not a field mouse! The voice came from *under* the ground."

Mrs Platt stared at her husband. "You don't say! *Go* on!"

"The little squeaking voice said words I understood," said Platt.

"Never!"

"It did! It spoke words and I heard them. I listened just as you are now, and just as that cat of yours is listening," Platt said indignantly.

"What nonsense! Puss isn't listening. But get on with your tale. What did the voice say, although I can't believe a word of this nonsense," she told him.

"Whether you believe it or not, I'm going to tell you," decided Platt and he trimmed his voice to a little high squeak and piped...

"Hey, you, Platt!
Tell your cat
Kurremurre is dead."

Platt took a deep breath and then said in his own voice, "Now why would our cat want to know a thing like that? Who is this Kurremurre, I'd like to know? Have you heard of him? Of course, not! I tell you, the whole thing doesn't make sense."

But oh, it did to Katto! He moved in such a hurry the saucer with its meat scraps spun away from under his foot and crashed against the peat bucket as Katto whooped about the kitchen. Then, up on his hind legs he stood to jig and twirl in the spilt broth and meat.

"Kurremurre is dead!" he sang.

"Kurremurre is dead!
Thank you for food!
Thank you for bed!
But come this night
And I'll be wed!"

He bowed to Platt and his Goody and with a great leap, Katto was up and out of the window and loping towards the dwarfs' hill, with his tail sticking up like a plume behind him.

Platt and his wife looked after Katto. "Did you ever see the like?" said Platt softly.

"No, I never!" murmured his Goody. "I wonder who our cat will wed?"

And maybe they never knew unless someone told them this story.

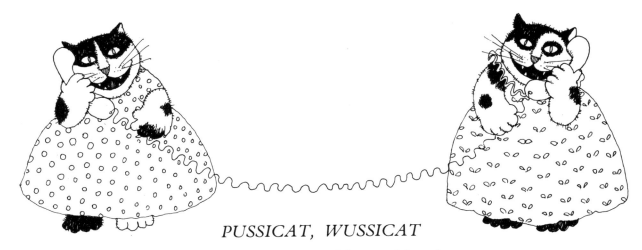

PUSSICAT, WUSSICAT

Pussicat, Wussicat with a white foot,
When is your wedding and I'll come to it?
The beer's to brew and the bread's to bake,
Pussicat, Wussicat, don't be late.

ROLL-ABOUT TROLLS

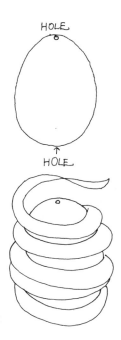

HOLE

HOLE

Each troll is made from the shell of a blown egg. Perhaps someone could help you to do this. Pierce a hole at either end of the egg. Gently blow through one hole, letting the egg yolk and its white slip into a clean container. It can be used later in cooking.

Carefully cover the egg with strips of tissue paper which have been dipped into paste, or glue. Add layer after layer, keeping the surface as smooth as possible.

Let the egg dry.
Cut a small hole through the top of the egg.
Partly fill the egg with tiny stones, sand, lead shot or something small and heavy.
Re-seal the egg.
It can be covered with another piece of tissue if you think it needs strengthening further.
Paint the egg with poster paints. Give it a troll face.
The weight inside the doll will help the toy to re-gain its balance when it's pushed over.

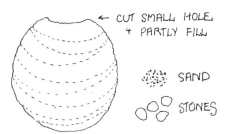

← CUT SMALL HOLE
+ PARTLY FILL

SAND

STONES

149

LOVE SOMEBODY

Love some - bod - y yes I do; Love some - bod - y,

yes I do; Love some - bod - y, yes I do;

Love some - bod - y, but I won't tell who.

GIVE A HEART

Birthday card? Christmas card? Christmas tree decoration?
A mobile for a window? Weave a heart and please someone
at gift time. You need two pieces of contrasting coloured
papers. Red and white, or your favourite colour combina-
tions.

Cut two pieces
in this shape,
using two colours.

Cut along the dotted
lines, making strips.
Be careful not to cut
too far.

Weave the slitted ends together. One colour over
the other, then under. The uncut rounded ends of
the paper become the curves of the heart and are a
space to write a message, or to decorate.

The hearts look well in see-through papers, patterned and
plain papers combined, or in textured papers, or one colour.
Experiment and become an expert heart maker.

LORD OF THE GOLDEN UMBRELLAS

The Lord of the Golden Umbrellas, the Wearer of the Crown Shaped like a Temple, the Keeper of the Most Majestic White Elephant, the Wearer of Jade and Pearls, was none other than the King of Siam and he loved his royal cat. She was the colour of clotted cream and her paws were browner than cinnamon, and her eyes were bluer than any corner of the sunlit sky. She sat with elegance upon her silken cushion. She supped from her bowl of beaten silver patterned with jewel-bright enamels. She slept upon the royal pillow and wore a golden necklace. Linked to her necklace was another chain of gold which the King kept looped about a finger. She was his most treasured possession and he called her, Precious One.

And she was indeed a valuable cat! Precious One could advise her King upon the affairs of his kingdom, on the growth of his children, a colour for a new robe, a gift for a favourite wife, or food for a feast. And she knew when to speak seriously and when to chat and gossip. All the people of the land knew of Precious One's wisdom, yet, when the King fell ill, no one thought to consult his cat.

The doctors said, "It is the heat of the summer which has sickened the Lord of the Golden Umbrellas." And they advised him to sit in a glass room which was to be lowered into the lake. "It will be cool in the room and you can watch the fish swim by," they told him.

152

However, this treatment did not improve the King's health. As each day passed he grew paler and weaker. The doctors shook their heads. "Someone must be poisoning His Majesty," they whispered. "Set guards to watch over the royal goblet and His Majesty's golden plate."

Now the King had many wives and each wife loved him well. They took it upon themselves to guard his food and drink. Alas, all fell asleep during the early hours of the morning, when the dark of night turned to the pale grey of dawn. And alas, the King's health grew worse. It was likely that he would die.

"I will guard my Lord of the Golden Umbrellas," spoke up Precious One. "I shall watch over his goblet and his plate."

"You will not be able to stay awake," the doctors said. "You sleep more often than a person. That is the habit of a cat, even one as noble as yourself."

"Trust me," said Precious One. "Trust me!"

She sprang to the table to lie close to the goblet and the plate. And she stayed awake all through that day and through the night. She stayed awake the next day and then another night. It was near to dawn when her eyelids slipped over her weary eyes. It was for a moment only. Precious One shook herself awake.

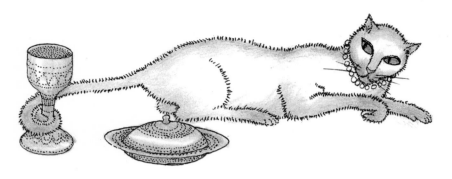

Again and again her eyes all but closed. She forced them to open wide, fixing her gaze on the goblet and plate. If only she could take a cat-nap, a brief cat-nap to refresh her weariness.

Now, Precious One was wise as well as beautiful, you will remember. And she uncurled her long tail which had been wrapped about her feet. She twisted its brown tip about the stem of the golden goblet and she held it tightly, very tightly. Then Precious One slept. No one dared to reach for the goblet. No one dared approach the golden plate. Precious One would have awakened at once to claw at the wicked hand.

And so days went by. Nights went by. Precious One still clung to the goblet and as each day passed the Lord of the Golden Umbrellas grew stronger. Soon he was completely well from his serious illness. "Precious One has saved our lord from death by poison," declared the doctors.

It was never discovered who was trying to kill the King.

"The evil person must have left the kingdom by this time," his wives believed. "Precious One no longer needs to guard the royal goblet and the golden plate."

The King lifted his cat from the table and placed her in his lap. He stroked down her neck, down her back, down her tail. "What has happened to your tail, Oh Precious One?" asked the King. "It's tip is now crooked."

"That is of no consequence, my Lord," she mewed, knowing that the long hours grasping the goblet had spoilt the beauty of her tail. "Let us not think upon it," she purred.

And her tail tip stayed slightly curved. No amount of smoothing or stroking would straighten it. The same little crooked tip appeared on the tails of Precious One's kittens and every kitten born into the Royal Siamese Cat Family since. You may see such a tail, if you know a cat like Precious One. That same cat will have the grace of a tiger, the sweetness of a lovebird, the beauty of a deer, the quickness of lightning and the wisdom of an elephant. So it is said in Siam.

CATTY SAYINGS

Here's a handful of sayings which have grown from people's interest in cats and knowing them well.

Cat burglar: a thief who enters by climbing. The burglar may wear a cat-suit which is a skin-fitting garment like leotards and made from black material. Why, do you think?

Cat call: a whistle often rude.

Curiosity killed the cat: is said about people who will not mind their own business.

Cats' concert: a horrible noise like cats singing.

Copy cat: someone who copies someone else.

Cat's eye: can be a kind of glass marble, or a semi-precious stone from Ceylon which looks like a cat's eye.

Cat's foot: an ivy creeper with leaves shaped like a cat's paw.

Fat cat: is someone who lives well without doing much work.

Looking like the cat who swallowed a canary: is said when someone looks very, very pleased.

Cat nap: a short sleep, often taken after a meal.

Cat nip: a small grey plant with blue flowers.

Cat and mouse game: when two people will not make a move.

Cat's paw: when someone is used as a tool by another person.

Let the cat out of the bag: is to speak of a secret matter.

No room to swing a cat: means that there is little space for movement.

Cat's pyjamas: is said when something very pleasant happens.

She's the cat's mother: is said when a person is not named and it would be polite to do so.

Scaredy cat: is just someone who is easily frightened.

Something the cat brought in: is mostly said about something which is not pleasant.

Raining cats and dogs: just means very heavy rain.

Cat walk: is the name given to a narrow bridge, or a narrow platform such as the ones where fashion parades may be held.

Cat's whiskers: usually means that something is very good, or pleasant.

Pussy-footing: is to walk very softly like a cat.

What other sayings do you know? Do they remind you of the way a cat behaves?

157

PUSS IN BOOTS

When a Miller died in a certain province in France, he left nothing to his youngest son but a cat. "My brothers can earn their living by running the mill together," said the lad. "When I've eaten my cat and used its fur to make a muff, I shall just have to starve."

"Not at all!" said the Cat. "Just give me a sack and a pair of boots so that I may go into the brambles. You'll soon find that you're not badly off, boy!"

Now the Cat had always been clever. He could hang upside-down by his feet, or lie as if dead in a flour bin and trick the rats and mice into becoming his dinner. So his young master gave him the things he wanted.

The Cat buckled on his boots, slung the bag over his shoulder and standing up on his hind legs, minced off to a nearby rabbit warren. He tucked some thistles into the sack, lay down as if he were dead and didn't move a whisker until some young rabbits poked their noses into the sack. Puss pulled a drawstring tightly and tied it into a knot, capturing the rabbits. He was so pleased with himself he decided to visit the King.

When he was taken before His Majesty, Puss bowed low, saying, "Sire, here is a plump rabbit. A gift from my lord, the Marquis of Carabas!"

The King received the Marquis' gift with pleasure, little knowing that the Marquis of Carabas was the name Puss had given to his master at that moment. And the King was to be pleased again another day when Puss arrived with two partridges tricked into his sack.

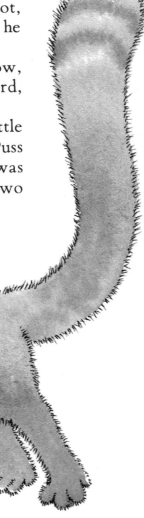

And for two or three weeks Puss took game to the palace, declaring that it had come from the Marquis' hunting grounds.

Then, the Cat heard that His Majesty planned to drive along the river bank with his daughter, who was the most lovely Princess in the world.

"Master," said Puss, "if you do as I say, your fortune will be made. Now, you must bathe in the river, and that is all. I'll attend to the rest."

The young Marquis did as his Cat ordered and there he was, up to his neck in river water when the King and his party came by. "Help!" shrieked Puss. "Help! Help! My Master's drowning!"

The King recognised the Cat. He ordered his guards to save the Marquis while Puss came crying to the carriage door. "Alas, alas! Thieves have stolen my Master's clothes!"

Of course, it was Puss who had taken the clothes. He had hidden them under a boulder! And the King, kindness itself, sent an officer back to the palace to fetch clothing suitable for the young Marquis. And when he was dressed in them he looked as handsome as any Prince. The Princess fell madly in love with him.

The King insisted that the Marquis should now drive with the royal carriage and Puss, pleased to see that his plot was working as he had planned it, ran on ahead of the carriage. He ran until he came to men mowing a meadow. "Dear good Mowers!" purred Puss. "If you do not tell the King that the meadow belongs to the Marquis of Carabas then I'll have you chopped up into cats' meat."

None of the mowers fancied that end and when the King passed and he asked, "Who owns this fine meadow, my good people?" "The Marquis of Carabas!" answered the mowers like a chorus.

Puss ran ahead again until he came to men harvesting a field. "Dear good Harvesters!" he purred. "If you do not tell the King that this field belongs to the Marquis of Carabas then I shall have you turned into sausages."

None of the harvesters fancied that end and when the King passed and asked, "Who owns this fine field, my good people?" The harvesters answered like a chorus, "The Marquis of Carabas, Your Majesty!"

Puss ran on ahead again and again. He threatened and he instructed the people he met how to answer their King.

And of course, the King was astonished that his guest, the Marquis of Carabas, owned such a fine estate of villages and meadows and fields. He congratulated the young man, who must have been confused by these claims.

In truth, the land belonged to a wicked ogre and Puss had heard this. And what did the Cat do but call upon the ogre to pay his respects.

"Take a seat," the ogre told Puss.

"Thank you," said Puss politely, making himself comfortable. "I have heard, Sir, that you have the power to change yourself into any kind of animal you wish. Can you actually become an elephant, or a lion?"

"That is so," the ogre grumbled gruffly. "I'll show you. I'll turn into a lion."

And he did. Puss was so scared when the lion appeared he sprang to the roof, and not without danger either because

his boots were not suitable for walking on tiles. "You *did* give me a fright!" he mewed down when the ogre changed back into his giant shape. "You are indeed, very clever, Sir!" Puss went on. "Now I am wondering if you also have the power to turn yourself into a small animal. A rat, or a mouse perhaps? That seems to be far more difficult to me. Impossible, I dare say."

"Impossible! Stuff and nonsense!" bellowed the ogre. "You shall see, you shall see!" And at once the ogre became a mouse. Puss watched him scurry across the floor, then he sprang, caught the mouse and ate it.

Meantime, the King had reached the ogre's castle and turned into it. As the carriage clattered over the draw-bridge Puss ran out to greet the party. "Welcome, Your Majesty! Welcome to the castle of the Marquis of Carabas!" he said with a deep bow.

"And a fine castle it is," answered the King. "Let us enter."

The Marquis offered his arm to the Princess and they followed the King and Puss up the steps to a great hall. A magnificent feast awaited them. It had been prepared for the ogre who had invited friends to dine, but none of them dared to appear when they heard that the King was present. And the King was delighted with Puss' arrangements, which he believed were to honour him.

And yes, the Marquis of Carabas seemed to be a most suitable husband for his lovely daughter. "You have only to say the word, my dear Marquis," he whispered, "and you may become my son-in-law. I will gladly give you my daughter's hand."

Of course, the Marquis accepted the King's offer. He had fallen in love with the Princess. They were married that same day. Puss became a Lord and from then on, only hunted for mice as a relaxation, if you can believe a word of it all.

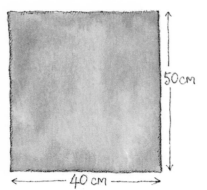

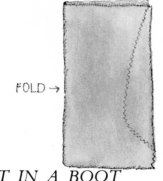

50cm

FOLD →

CUT OUTLINE OF BOOT

← 40 CM →

CAT IN A BOOT

This boot works best if it is made from felt.

The felt should be 40cm x 50cm. You'll need some contrasting felt, braid for trimming and some embroidery thread.

Fold the felt into two. Make the edges as even as you can. The fold will become one side of the boot.

Cut a boot shape with pinking shears if you have any. You may be wise to first make a pattern from newspaper so that your boot is well-shaped.

Open out the felt boot. It is easier to decorate the boot at this stage.

Cut a cat shape from the contrasting felt. Again use a newspaper pattern to help you. Its features can be embroidered.

Position the cat on the boot and stitch it into place. Use tacking threads to guide you.

Decorate the cat with embroidery and braid.

Trim the top of the boot with braid.

Stitch the sides of the boot together with firm stitches. You could use wool in a contrasting colour.

Sew a tag on the boot so that it can be hung as a Christmas stocking, or as a storage place for small treasure, even socks if the boot is a large one.

Put out the cat!
And lock the door!
Pick up your things
From off the floor!
Then wash your feet
And clean your teeth;
Put out the light
And say goodnight!

Sleep tight!

The moon shines bright,
The stars give light,
Little Pussy Leather-nose
Has come to say goodnight!

167

INDEX

Anything for Fish	52	Long Time Ago	105
At-Choom!	31	Lord of the Golden Umbrellas	152
Barnyard Song	48	Love Somebody	150
Beans in a Bag	112	Magic Ring, The	115
Belling the Cat	42	Monkey Business	104
Bells of London, The	143	Mother Shuttle	30
Boy Who Drew Cats, The	97	Most Beautiful and	
Cat	20	Most Precious	16
Cat and Dog Game	119	Mouse-Hound	127
Cat Bath	29	Nancy's Cat	75
Cat Came Back, The	113	Nine Lives	50
Cat Comfort	36	Noah's Ark	67
Cat in a Boot	166	Old Grey Cat, The	43
Cat Naps	37	Old Mother Mitchell	132
Cat Toys	20	Owl and the Pussy-Cat, The	110
Cats' Cradle	15	Peanut Puppets	90
Cat's Dinner, The	51	Pillowcase Cat	41
Cats' Eyes	95	Place by the Fire, A	32
Cat's Pyjamas	38	Puppet Witch	90
Catty Sayings	156	Puss in Boots	158
Clever Tom	102	Pussicat, Wussicat	149
Clickity-Click!	80	Pussy Wants a Corner	35
Clucky Hen	50	Ring-a-Ling!	140
Conversation in the		Roll-about Trolls	149
Middle of the Night	40	Rooster King	44
Devil-Mouse	64	Rose is Red, The	109
Dick Whittington	133	Six Little Mice	126
Ding-Dong!	142	Sock Puppet	91
Draw or Paint	101	Spell for Good Luck, A	88
Fat Cat	56	Spring is Coming	11
Fun-Mouse	121	Swish Goes the Broomstick!	83
Give a Heart	151	Tabby Teasers	22
Here is the Sea	55	Tailor Mouse	123
I Know an Old Lady	62	Tails	74
Juba	94	There Was a Crooked Man	120
Kilkenny Cats	91	Tillica	25
Kitty Alone	24	Two Red, Round Cakes	92
King Solomon's Ring	106	Velvet Paws	84
Knitting Nancy	79	Wash First, Then Eat	26
Kurremurre	144	Where's Your Tail, Pussy?	68
Little Bird	19	Witch's Brew	89
		Wondrous Thing, A	12